"Secrets" of
Effective Offense

Also by Marc MacYoung

Becoming a Complete Martial Artist
with Tristan Sutrisno and Dianna Gordon

"Secrets" of
Effective Offense

Survival Strategies for Self-Defense, Martial Arts, and Law Enforcement

Marc MacYoung

The Lyons Press
Guilford, Connecticut
An imprint of The Globe Pequot Press

The Lyons Press is an imprint of The Globe Pequot Press.

10 9 8 7 6 5 4 3 2 1

Printed in the United States of America

Photographs by Page Alcorta, Jesse Alcorta, and Doug Wittrock

Library of Congress Cataloging-in-Publication Data

MacYoung, Marc.
    Secrets of effective offense: survival strategies for self-defense, martial arts, and law enforcement / Marc MacYoung.
        p. cm.
    Includes Index.
    ISBN 1-59228-369-1 (trade cloth)
    1. Martial arts. 2. Hand-to-hand fighting, Oriental Offense. 3. Self-defense. I. Title.

GV1101.M23 2004
796.86dc22   2004048754

As always for my wife,
Dianna Gordon MacYoung,
whose love helped me finally walk away
from the edge of the abyss

If I have seen farther than others,
it is because I have stood
upon the shoulders of giants.

—Sir Isaac Newton

Contents

Foreword

One of the biggest mistakes you can make when either attacking or defending is to put your faith in one specific technique. No single maneuver will save you—not a specific punch, kick, grab, gouge, claw, scratch, or takedown. No, it is *you*—what *you* do at the right time—along with the right technique, that will save your life.

This is one of the essential principles that Marc MacYoung presents in this fundamental and stimulating book. Marc explains how it takes both intelligence and physical acuity to create an effective warrior. That's right, boys and girls, despite what many people might think about martial artists or law enforcement officers—that they are people who have chosen to develop physically, but have painfully little associated mental acuity—just the opposite is true.

Marc's focus on using your head is evident in his discussion of strategy. In fact, it is what makes his message unique. Strategy is defined by *Webster's New World Dictionary* as "the science of planning and directing large-scale military operations, or a plan of action based on this." What does this mean for you? While we aren't talking about a large-scale military operation, we *are* talking about planning for action.

An effective plan of action involves using the totally integrated person to either defend oneself from an attack or to launch an offense appropriately, according to Marc. He discusses the importance of integrating key components into this plan, including the ability to have one's priorities straight.

Priorities become very important when you consider that in the realm of fighting, as in so many other areas of life, "complex situations arise because of multiple factors," as Marc observes. In other words, whatever might go wrong in a critical situation often does.

As an experienced martial artist, I have encountered many books, martial artists, and defense instructors who have spent an inordinate amount of time defending specific techniques and movements to the exclusion of others, in a quest to establish their own style's uniqueness and supposed superiority. This practice has hindered the development of potential in many fine martial artists. *Effective Offense* places this pursuit of the "perfect" martial arts system right where it should be: in the same category as the pursuit of the Holy Grail. In other words, a perfect system is a great idea and would be nice if it existed, but might we not spend our precious time on this earthly plane more productively, such as in learning how to do something that works?

Marc shows how the disciplined application of priorities, skills, and techniques by a thinking and feeling martial artist can be combined in a logical and productive manner to help develop an effective defense. As you will find from his writing, it is not the pursuit of techniques that alone makes an *effective offense* work; it is the application of enduring fundamental principles that will move you to a higher level of knowledge and proficiency in your studies, whether of martial arts or defensive tactics. This book will show you how to become a more effective and efficient martial artist.

In training we often reach plateaus. We find ourselves feeling stuck, unable to convince our bodies, minds, or creativity to help us reach the next level. The information in this book will help you to become unstuck by moving you to a higher level of awareness, at which you can develop a unique and effective offense.

Having trained, taught, and learned with Marc MacYoung, I can say that if you are going to buy one martial arts book this year, this is the one to buy.

Joseph P. Bablonka, Ph.D.
6th Dan, Chun Kuk Moo Sul
(Universal Fighting Arts Fellowship International)

Introduction

A nation that will insist on drawing a broad line of demarcation between the fighting man and the thinking man, will have its fighting done by fools and its thinking done by cowards.

—Sir William Francis Butler

Among experienced fighters there is a joke: *Murphy was an optimist.*

If knowledgeable people tell you that "anything that can go wrong will" is being optimistic, it is a sure bet that you are about to open a serious can of worms. Effective offense is a complex and variable problem. It is made even more difficult because your opponent isn't cooperating. He is, in fact, doing everything in his power to foil you.

His interference is a part of what makes it complicated, but it isn't all of it—it isn't even a majority of it. His resistance serves to dramatically reveal the real problem. And that is that what you are trying to do is probably flawed.

What you are trying to do is not "wrong" per se, that is too strong a word, but rather it is missing critical components. That makes it flawed.

Unfortunately, these "flaws" are not normally revealed until you are in a crisis. It's like discovering multiple holes in your life raft while abandoning a sinking ship. This is not the time for you to discover extra complications.

There are components that make things work and their absence will cause no end of problems. But the good news is "flawed" still means *fixable*. This does not mean, however, that you can fix an absence by doing what created that absence, but doing it harder, faster, and with more extreme attitude. You don't get out of a hole by digging faster.

What it does mean is you can fix the problem by putting back the missing components. But to do that, you must step back and look at the bigger picture. With that in mind, I want to introduce you to a fundamental of this book:

Complex situations arise because of multiple factors.

Knowing these factors, their significance, and how to balance them allows a person to cope with complex situations. As I will discuss later, how well you combine them is at the very least a skill, but more often an art.

Because multiple factors cannot be fully addressed by any one solution, there are no simple "just do this" answers to the challenge of effective offense. While a single technique might provide guidelines, it really is only a way to manifest certain principles. These principles may—or may not—apply to the situation at hand. Even if they do, the odds are slim that a given technique will work without its being "tweaked" slightly for the situation.

But before you can effectively tweak something, you must understand how it works in the first place. While understanding *why* it works is preferable, *how* is often good enough. Knowing how will assist you in creating the proper tweaks to make it work.

With this background, I want to emphasize that anyone who offers you a "guaranteed" response is appealing to your laziness. No one can teach "prepackaged" responses that always work. There ain't no such critter. You have to make effective tweaks on the spot. They must be tailored to the circumstances surrounding that exact moment. And make no mistake, those circumstances are always changing.

Sound complicated? It is.

However, like all complicated tasks, this one looks overwhelming only if you try to tackle it all at once, instead of in bite-sized pieces. As my late father-in-law was wont to say, life's hard by the yard, but a cinch by the inch. The same can be said about learning effective offense. If you have been taught complex, "yard-long" techniques, the odds are that you have had some bad experiences in which they have failed. The approach I would like to take is in "inches," making sure that each small component is nailed down before trying to move on. In the final analysis, a yard is made up of inches. If you don't have all the smaller parts in place, you are going to fall short.

The good news is that the elements involved in mounting an effective offense are constant, and often quite simple. This book will help you to identify these "inch-long" elements, then assist you in learning how to design effective responses and solutions on the spot—that is, help you develop a skill.

The intent of the book is to give you not the *answers* but the *tools*, with tips on using them. As I tell my students, "You have to know how to do this on your own, because if you get into a fight, I won't be standing there coaching you." By the time you finish this book you will know how to generate an effective offense. The only remaining task will be to practice in order to achieve new standards of proficiency.

I would like to offer a suggestion that will help you gain the maximum benefit from this book: Do not apply this information to any self-defense system with which you are familiar. In other words, avoid trying to make this information "fit" into what you already know. Instead, seek to apply what you already know to the larger ideas that the book describes. See how what you know fits into the bigger picture.

I would also advise against trying to digest all of the book's information in one gulp. To obtain the book's full value, you may have to read it several times. I've poured my 35 years of experience into it, and that's a lot to absorb in a single pass.

~ 1 ~

Basics and Fundamentals

*You cannot resolve significant problems
with the same thinking that created them.*

—Albert Einstein

In this book I will give you "building codes" for offense. In order to do this, I must first beg your indulgence and ask you to participate in a paradigm shift. This shift will allow you to look at a bigger picture regarding what is needed for effective offense. Once you see the bigger picture, you will never look at your training in the same way again.

What are the building codes of offense? These are the standards that an offense must meet in order to be "effective." By effective, I don't just mean that they work against a specific type of opponent and under specialized circumstances. I mean that they work reliably and consistently, under a wide spectrum of conditions and against a wide variety of opponents. These are the standards that your strategy—no matter what it is—must meet if you are to have long-term success.

Fighters tend to find a particular strategy or rely on a particular element that is successful in the kinds of situations they

1

encounter. These strategies or elements tend to work *for that individual* and under limited circumstances. For example, in a fight, size does matter, and it can be used to one's advantage. Therefore, a large fighter is likely to rely on his size and strength to carry the day. He often will rely on mass and muscle to compensate for poor technique. These elements indeed often succeed against a smaller, weaker opponent, especially in minor scuffles. Believing that size assures success, the large fighter may settle for his current skill level and focus his training efforts on enhancing that advantage (e.g., through weight-lifting). This won't make him a better fighter, just a bigger and stronger one. I have met many followers of "reality-based" fighting schools who fail to realize that it is their excellent physical condition not their fighting skills or the effectiveness of their system that grants them victory.

While enhancing one's size and strength might look like a winning strategy, off the top of my head I can name at least four situations in which it will fail: 1) against a weapon, 2) against a smaller, trained fighter who knows better than to contest superior mass, 3) against a larger, strong opponent, and 4) against an opponent of equal size and strength. The first two won't entail minor scuffles, but serious, possibly deadly, encounters. The fighter who relies on size had better hope that the third situation involves a minor scuffle because he is otherwise in line for a beating. The fourth will take the form of a knock-down, drag-out fight with an unpredictable outcome.

In other words, as long as the "big guy" carefully chooses his fights, he will win by using a strategy based on his size and physical condition.

Still sound good? The reality is that you don't always get to choose who you go up against. Sooner or later, you are going to face someone with an effective counter for your pet strategy.

This is especially true if it is your job to draw the line and say no to troublemakers. Then it isn't a matter of *if* it will happen, but of *when*. And when it happens, you had better have something other than size or strength up your sleeve. Ideally, you would have a more reliable strategy in the first place—one that can counter your opponent's tactics, no matter what they may be.

The bottom line is that in order for a strategy to be effective, it must meet a wide range of criteria. It must work under a wide spectrum of circumstances. It must *not* depend on the size and strength of either party. Most important, it must work even if you unexpectedly find yourself facing weapons.

Sound complicated? It is and it isn't.

Effective offense is about having your priorities straight and making sure that you accomplish them.

If your initial strategy works, you won't have to rely on a backup plan, which by definition is never as effective as your initial one. The task at hand is to understand your priorities and how to accomplish them. You must learn how to do this under normal conditions before practicing under stressful ones. You can't just jump in and try to apply these principles and priorities when you clash with someone. Once you realize how important they are, you will put them into your initial strategy and thus increase the chances of its working in the first place— even under stress. This means having your ducks in a row beforehand, not trying to get them in line in the middle of a live-fire situation.

Creating effective solutions to complicated problems looks easy when you have done a lot of prior work; not just practice, but "homework," i.e., learning the ideas involved in effective strategy, knowing when to apply them, and creating them under stress. To accomplish this, you need to know something other than just "techniques" and do a lot more than get in the ring and bang with someone.

You need to know the rules and laws that underlie the techniques and their use. Following those rules will allow you to effectively apply those techniques.

Let me draw an analogy. Even if you are an experienced carpenter, you can't just go out and build a house. You have to do some planning. If you don't want the house to collapse on your head, you have to learn a thing or two about architecture. Electricity and plumbing are other things you must know something about.

To organize the project into a working whole, you have to read and understand the building codes. What you design and build must meet these codes. That is where "the rubber meets the road"; if it doesn't meet code, it ain't happening. As a fighter, consider your opponent a building inspector with a really bad attitude who is just looking for the smallest excuse to put a kibosh on your project.

It is important to realize that building codes aren't made up just to annoy you. Their rationale incorporates laws and principles relating to how things really work. The codes cover a variety of problems that you might not have thought about. They seek to prevent buildings from collapsing, blowing up, catching on fire, or rotting away, for example. The codes—without going into the physics behind them—provide guidelines for the design and construction of a solid, secure building, consistent with the laws and principles of physics, stability, and safety.

If you fail to meet these codes, you will have problems, especially if you will be the one who is living in that house.

Taking this analogy a bit further, how you meet these standards, how you design for the location and the environment has less to do with your skill as a carpenter than with your skill as an architect. The hammer-swinging carpenter is at the end of a long chain that connects other skills and areas of knowledge. Those other skills determine what the carpenter builds.

The same idea applies to offense. Using any particular "technique" is like swinging a hammer. If it does not represent the end of a longer process, you are headed for trouble. Before you swing a hammer, you need to have a well-thought-out design, which in turn requires that you know what is involved in a good design. This is what I mean when I say that an effective offense looks easy only when you have done a lot of work beforehand, i.e., studied the "building codes" and practiced meeting them. This is how you become acquainted with the *standards and priorities of what you must do.*

I am not talking about any particular technique, but about making sure that whatever technique you use meets the standards of effective offense. If it doesn't, then, as in the case of not building to code, all kinds of things will go wrong. Remember, your opponent isn't on your side. He is, in fact, actively seeking to ruin your efforts. Like a building inspector with an ax to grind, he is trying to shut you down. If you don't meet code, he will succeed.

Two major problems complicate learning the building codes of effective offense. The first concerns instruction. For most people training in martial arts, self-defense, or defensive tactics revolves around technique. This approach doesn't include "design" (read: application). Most students learn a technique, with no real understanding of when to use it or what must be present for it to meet "code." Knowledge about how to use such techniques comes from stepping into a sparring ring and learning by getting hit—not by receiving effective guidelines. This approach often results in a hodgepodge of partial understanding.

Sticking with the building analogy, what is commonly taught as offense is "carpentry." Such instruction assumes that by doing enough carpentry, a thorough knowledge of "architecture" will follow. Put simply, one learns by doing. This is neither effective teaching nor a precise way to learn architecture, however. It definitely isn't an effective way to teach offense. While the teacher *might* be able to make the moves work, it is not likely students will be able to make a full and correct intuitive leap to application until after many years of practice. This leaves the students vulnerable to being "shut down" by opponents because they don't know how to "meet code" in the real world.

The second problem concerns the students' assumptions. One of the worst is that all they need to learn is technique—which, after all, is what they are being taught. It is naïve but common to assume that knowing the technique is enough. With that assumption, the student is not likely to keep learning about the building codes, much less how to meet them. This is the equivalent of saying that all you need to know about military strategy is how to fire your M-16. Technique is an important part of effective offense, but there is much more.

This emphasis on technique leads to both a serious and, unfortunately, common problem. After trying to apply the technique in a live-fire situation and failing miserably, the student will no longer trust the technique. In high-risk professions, this distrust can and often does extend to any further defensive-tactics training. This can result in an overreliance on authority and firearms, which is dangerous to both the student and anyone he encounters in conflict. In a nonprofessional contest, it can result in a hazardous overreliance on attributes like attitude or physical conditioning.

To understand where I am going with all of this, you must realize that techniques are prepackaged, general responses to commonly encountered problems.

Techniques are manifestations of important principles. They are not the principles themselves. In order to apply them correctly, you must understand the principles they represent. These principles are the "building codes" I am talking about. While techniques *should* contain the fundamentals, even if they do, they are not themselves the whole solution. And I need to warn you that many techniques I have seen taught as *self-defense* have been modified for sporting or legal purposes. They may not contain the principles of effective offense anymore. Therefore, they are unreliable for self-defense, much less as control tactics.

The assumption I must constantly warn students about is: Just because you know a technique doesn't mean you understand how to apply it. Put in simple terms, just because you know it doesn't mean you can do it.

I say that because very seldom will a technique work in a live-fire situation without tweaks and minor changes. It is your knowledge of these principles (or codes) that allows you to effectively tweak a technique according to the circumstances.

What further complicates this situation is that most techniques are actually a combination of many elements, but with very little emphasis on priorities. While the fundamentals might be present, without specific instruction as to their importance you might get lost in the details of the move instead of focusing on the more important task of meeting the standards that will make it effective. You lose the priorities of the move.

I cannot tell you how many times I have seen techniques fail. And those techniques were technically perfect—according to how they were taught in the dojo. What they failed to do is meet the goal of the move. The reason they failed is that the individual was too busy focusing on minor details to make sure that he satisfied the priorities.

This is the difference between doing it "right" and meeting code. And meeting code is very much an issue of priorities and emphasis. You can do it exactly as you were taught in the dojo and still not meet code. How you position your hand during a throw is far, far less important than making sure you break your attacker's balance. Your focus needs to be on the priority, disrupting his balance, not on whether you are holding your palm up, grasping his shirt, or holding your palm down.

How widespread is this problem of not addressing priorities? I have seen wars between schools of the same martial arts style over the right way to perform a technique. These intense rivalries are over what are, functionally, minor details—variations that have no clearly demonstrable advantage or disadvantage. They both work—and fail—to the same degree.

Unfortunately, I have most often seen that neither school's version meets the building codes of the move. For example, if the standard for a block is "don't get hit," then both versions fail miserably. Neither version reliably keeps the student from getting hit. It seems that the higher the failure rate, the greater the intensity of the debate over the right way to do the move.

This is what I mean by details versus priorities. What standards does a technique have to meet in order for it to work in an altercation? That is the difference between art and application. In effective offense, it is all about application—not art. It is about meeting priorities, not details. You may be doing the move exactly right, according to what you were taught, but if what you are doing doesn't meet the standards (building codes), it will fail in a live-fire situation against an aggressive opponent.

This problem is exacerbated if elements of your solution are poorly understood or wrongly applied. While this is true of any complex situation, it especially applies to effective offense. You can understand how to drive a nail and have everything ready and in a position to do it, but if your hammer is broken you have a problem. The same can be said if you try to drive a nail with a wrench. These *failures to perform*—in the midst of an already complex situation—often prove to be overwhelming. In simple terms, all the theory in the world isn't going to help you if you can't deliver a good, powerful punch, kick, or other offensive maneuver.

Let's sum up the problems we have thus far discussed. First, most currently available training is oriented toward techniques, with the assumption that you will figure out how to apply them as you go. This is the carpenter versus architect issue. Second, your opponent isn't about to give you time to figure out your mistakes. He is, in fact, actively trying to collapse your attempts at offense. Third, even if your offense gets through, if it doesn't meet code there is a good chance of its not working. It won't have enough power to work, and doing it harder won't make it work any better.

That's a pretty ugly situation. So how do we fix it?

The really good news is that many of the elements that will help you create an effective offense will also assist you in performing the nuts-and-bolts issues correctly.

As you can see by the building analogy, it is the blending of the theoretical (architectural design) with the practical (tools, supplies, and construction skills) that allows you to build a solid house. It isn't just one thing that makes an effective solution to complicated problems; it is myriad aspects that must work together. You must be architect, contractor, and carpenter all at once. You cannot specialize in just one field.

I understand that this may sound daunting, but in truth it isn't that hard—if you approach it from the right mind-set. That is why I asked you to engage in a paradigm shift. While complex situations usually do not have a single, simple solution, the elements needed to solve them are not necessarily difficult or individually complicated. In fact, they can be rather simple.

The complexity arises in their combination.

A major so-called secret of effective offense is *to be able to do several extremely simple things at once*. It is the combination and proportions of these elements that make for an efficacious result; not too much, not too little, but just the right mix for the situation.

The analogy I use to convey this idea of fundamentals and their combinations refers to something most people do every day: drive a car. This act consists of only three elements: steering, braking, and accelerating.[1] None of these elements is, in and of itself, particularly difficult. A basic ability to do each can be acquired through half an hour's practice in a parking lot.

However, *it is the combination of these three simple elements—in response to the circumstances at hand—that makes for the complexity of driving.*

In order to develop the "skill" of driving, you must be able to appropriately mix and match these three simple elements to create the right responses to ever-changing situations. The elements don't change, but their proportions do. If your combination is out of proportion for the circumstances, you will get into a wreck—even if that combination would have been perfect for another situation. Simply stated, you are still doing the same

---

1. Okay, in many cases there is a fourth—gearing—but let's use three for the moment, because whether you drive an automatic or stick often depends on where you live. Automatics are far more common in the U.S. while manuals are more common in Europe.

three things whether you are driving 25 or 120 mph, but you are doing them in different proportions.

This brings in an entirely different skill set, one that is not necessarily physical, but mental. These skills are awareness, knowledge, assessment, experience, training, and the ability to judge feedback. They are based on how you assess the situation and your knowledge to correctly mix the physical elements that are needed. This is how you create the correct response for the moment at hand. Then you apply that response.

In the next moment you are going to repeat the process and come up with a different combination.

When you can combine the physical elements with the mental aspects, you develop the *skill* of driving. Skill is learning how to take the theoretical and turn it into the practical—and doing it at the drop of a hat. The same goes for learning how to apply effective offense.

I want you to stop and consider the implications of that last paragraph. It is important because it should change how you look at learning (or teaching) the martial arts or defensive tactics. Using the driving analogy, I have shown you this is not an insurmountable task. You do this kind of thinking already. All you need to do now is start to apply it to your offensive tactics training.

This takes your thinking away from learning techniques and focuses it on learning the principles that allow you to apply them. Creating an effective offense is a skill—not a particular set of techniques.

And the only way to develop that skill is by practice—but a very specific form of practice. It must not only establish technical proficiency, but also be oriented toward teaching principles and developing skills of assessment, reaction, feedback, and judgment to work with those principles. In short, techniques must be an integrated part of a greater whole—not the whole, nor a stand-alone element, and most especially not esoteric or traditional dead weight. They must be part of a dynamic network that you control.

This takes the idea of a technique and moves it out of the context of a dead, robotic response. It is no longer a rote, "this is how you do it" response. It instead becomes a manifestation of principles and a living part of the whole, an instrumental part of achieving a greater goal. You are no longer trying to do something and hoping it has a desired effect. You are now using it as a clearly defined element to achieve a goal. Put simply, it isn't just a matter of "do this"; it is learning how to judge when, where, and how to do it.

To accomplish this you need to have that element—and all its variables—well and truly nailed down, to a point where you don't even have to think about the technical aspects anymore; you just do them appropriately.

A good way to understand what I am talking about is to go back to the driving analogy. Let's pick one element, braking, which will provide an example of what is involved in what I call a technical aspect. Just pushing the brake pedal down is not all there is to braking. Braking is also knowing how hard you must brake at different speeds in order to stop at certain distances.

This "basic" concept is far more complicated than one might imagine and must be practiced individually at first. It is often introduced to student drivers in empty parking lots. You must familiarize yourself with a great deal of information before you even consider the complexities involved in driving on the street or highway. Few people realize the amount of information that is absorbed by braking in the parking lot. The student driver must learn to *feel* the brakes and to judge stopping distance.

In time this will become an ingrained ability, one you don't even have to think about when you drive a familiar vehicle. It also is important to realize how this ability, once ingrained, can be expanded to different vehicles. The time it takes to learn the braking levels of the new vehicle will be minimal in comparison to how long it took to initially learn this ability, but at first you still must consciously focus on the change in conditions.

I cannot stress enough the importance of this way of learning. When you learn to drive, the importance of feedback is constantly emphasized. You don't learn to apply the brakes just by slamming on them every time. This helps to ingrain an understanding about the need for awareness, assessment, and judgment. These are skills you will acquire, and then constantly reinforce, through practice and experience.

To continue with the idea of training in a parking lot before attempting the street, this isolated (and conceptual) training allows the student to focus on individual aspects before attempting to combine them with others.

The same needs to be done when teaching offense. All that teaching a technique does is show students how to "slam on the brakes" every time. Once a student has learned how to isolate and apply fundamental elements, it is time to start teaching how to combine them, but only after the student has learned the significance and application of individual components.

The task at hand is to ingrain these fundamental elements individually before you try to combine them, much less apply them in adverse conditions.

When you know them individually, you can work on combining them within the move itself. Learning individual components and the practice of combining should be the first focus of your training. When you step into the sparring ring, don't think about "winning"; instead, focus on perfecting the combination of these elements under adverse conditions. If you win, fine. If you lose, who cares? You are a step closer to being able to blend these critical elements under stressful circumstances and make sure that they are always present in whatever you do. The ability to do these two things is critical for effective offense.

Eventually, the nature of your practice will change, toward learning how to effectively combine them under varying circumstances. This is the first of a two-phase process.

In order to be able to attack with proficiency, you must have a firm grasp of two aspects of training. The first is the technical aspect, i.e., how to correctly punch, kick, block, trap, and throw (by "correctly" I mean doing these in a way that delivers power). Then how to effectively combine them into a technique.

The second aspect of training is how to assess when to apply these techniques for optimum timing and efficiency—according to the immediate situation. You do this knowing that the circumstances will change in the next second, so it is an ongoing process of analysis.

Being able to do both of these is the definition of skill.

In truth, the division between these aspects is not that cut and dried. Technique and principle do blend into one another, as the braking analogy shows. For the purposes of this book, however, we will divide technical aspects and principles initially, so that you can understand the importance of each. Then we will proceed to recombine them.

Before we go any further, there is something I want to make clear: It is important that you not get hung up on these definitions and separations.

These explanations are for communication purposes and to acquaint you with ideas. You have to work with these ideas in order to understand their significance. I am not claiming that the model I am presenting is the Truth™ about fighting. I am saying that these are things that you must research and understand in order to be effective at offense.

How you define them is up to you. Use whatever model works best. I present this model because it easily explains the factors that need to be present for effective offense. I have found that it works well for most of the people whom I have taught. But always remember that a model isn't reality; or as we often say, the map isn't the territory.

This model or map is presented just to help you find your way. You must walk the territory yourself; just knowing the map isn't enough.

～ 2 ～

Defining the Problem

In all fighting, the direct method may be used for joining battle,
but indirect methods will be needed in order to secure victory. In
battle, there are not more than two methods of attack—the direct
and the indirect; yet these two in combination give rise to an
endless series of maneuvers. The direct and the indirect lead on to
each other in turn. It is like moving in a circle—you never come
to an end. Who can exhaust the possibilities of their combination?

—Sun Tzu, *The Art of War*

Fighting has been going on for a long time. While technological advances have caused major changes in certain aspects, other elements have remained relatively constant. The fact that humans have two arms, two legs, and other standard equipment has not changed—thus giving rise to the old saw that "there are only so many ways the human body moves."

The first challenge has always been to find ways for it to move more effectively in a conflict. The art and science of making that happen have been around for thousands of years. Since the basic design of humans hasn't changed much, recurring elements and problems have been encountered again and again.

These have been analyzed and discussed, and, unfortunately, the wheel has been reinvented many times. New strategies have replaced old because, for the moment, they worked. Then, even newer counters were developed, which foiled the "new" way. Often the process went full circle, in time returning to a "new" version of the old way. It might have taken a hundred or so years, but the result would have been recognizable to the original users of the old system. To the latest generation, however, it is completely novel.

What has changed dramatically is how we communicate this information.

Communication has always been the second major challenge. Teaching what you know, its implications, and its importance in certain circumstances, has always been the weak link in the chain. The elders knew it was a really good idea, but they couldn't communicate the realities of why it is important. The younger generation, which has never experienced combat, see no need for training—or underestimate its importance.

In our times, every few years some marketing guru comes up with a new way of explaining old information and presents the new "ultimate fighting" art or "guaranteed" tactical system. By reintroducing a "lost" fragment, the new fighting messiah enjoys incredible success. While thousands might flock to this new "system," there will always be detractors who rightfully claim, "We do that! Our stuff is just as good! That isn't anything new!"

To tell you the truth, they are more right than they can imagine, but for the wrong reasons.

When a Jeet Kun Do player explains to me what a genius Bruce Lee was for coming up with the concepts of angles, vectors, high line, and low line, I direct the player to fencing texts from the 16th and 17th centuries: DiGrassi, Agrippa, and

Vincentio Saviolo, to name a few sword fighting writers from that era. (But I also point them to George Silver's critiques of the same systems.) The ideas of angles and vectors were well known to fighters of 300 and 400 years ago, so these ideas are definitely not new.

It is from "fencing" that I draw an idea that I consider critical for effective offense. By fencing I don't mean the modern sport with toy swords, but rather the murderous art and science that men lived and died by throughout the ages. I do this in hopes of communicating an idea that has, in my opinion, been largely lost by most teachers of so-called fighting systems.

In the United States the word *defense* is spelled with an s, so what I am about to tell you is not as obvious. In other English-speaking countries, you will often see the word spelled d-e-f-e-n-c-e.

Four hundred years ago the term *art of fence* was used instead of the more modern *fencing.* The latter term is reputed to have been both a combination and shortening of two words, *offence* and *defence.* Your actions did both; ergo the word *fence* in *art of fence*, which eventually was shortened to its current form, *fencing.*

What is important is that art of fence *comprised both aspects in equal proportion.* It was oriented toward both effective offense and effective defense in combat. It meant not only putting your blade in the other fellow, but making sure he didn't do the same to you. This occurred at a time when combatants were not hindered by the modern sports context, with rules of right of way. What is interesting is how often, through positioning and movement, the art of fence achieved both aspects with the same move and at the same time.

Forgetting the artsy idea of fencing and its modern sports rules for a moment, let's looks at the practical. The ability to do this offense-defense combination is critical for effective offense

in a live-fire situation, as when dueling with a man who is holding what is functionally a three-foot straight razor and is trying to play show-and-tell with your vital organs. You must not only do unto him, but keep him from doing unto you.

In Japan at the end of the 1800s, a book was written on bushido. In it, Inazo Nitobe, the author, postulated that the highest level of swordsmanship and bushido was achieved when both swordsmen struck each other down at the same time. It is important to remember that the man who was writing this standard of samurai conduct lived during a period of 200 years of stability, brought about by the Tokugawa shogunate. It was not someone who had lived during the nearly 400 years of constant warfare that had racked medieval Japan. In other words, it wasn't an experienced soldier's opinion.

It is important to realize this because the idea of dying as a sign of skill would be ludicrous to anyone who had actually faced battle. In fact, most would tend to agree with General George S. Patton when he said, "No dumb son of a bitch ever won a war by dying for his country. You win a war by making some other poor dumb son of a bitch die for his."

Unfortunately, this idea of the bushido double-kill has infected most martial arts training. Practitioners go into a sparring match expecting to get hit. Therefore they don't do anything to prevent it—much less something that will assist them in bringing about a successful conclusion to the engagement. This is why I say that the concept of *fence* has been lost by most practitioners of martial arts and defensive tactics.

In order to begin to grasp the importance of fence, you must understand the concept of different levels (or types) of offense. The following is a rough model and should in no way be taken as carved in stone. It is just a way to communicate an important idea. Having said that, in the opening scenes of the movie *The Last Boy Scout*, a football player is told to get the touchdown "no matter what." Now football is a rough contact sport, where practice, special equipment, and strategies are critical elements for success. But everybody knows this and plays by the same rules.

The player, motivated by medication and a threatening telephone call telling him to score at all costs, decides to take it a little too far. As he runs toward the goal, another player rushes to tackle him. The ball carrier pulls out a pistol and shoots the tackler, then proceeds to shoot a few more individuals in order to score. His version of "no matter what" is far more serious than everyone else's. This scene goes miles toward explaining the difference between limited and unlimited offenses—and how fast things can go from one type to another.

There are three basic types of offense:

- Limited Offense
- Unlimited Offense
- Total Offense

Although this model only has three levels, there are different degrees within these levels. And these levels can go from personal to professional to national to global.

In their most simple form, sports are the prime example of limited offense. In more complicated versions you have police defensive tactics and even limited warfare (according to the Geneva convention). Understanding limited offense is very easy because there are rules.

These rules limit the type and nature of allowable attacks. These accepted standards determine and control offense. They also establish protocols, rituals, and even regulatory bodies. You cannot take a pistol into a football game, a cop cannot execute a suspect. Our country cannot drop a nuke on a country that our military leaders assume is harboring a terrorist leader. Such an action would violate the rules that define limited offense.

Limited offenses are the foundation of most modern sports, especially contact ones. You train for dealing with and creating limited offenses. Keep this concept in mind because it creates unconscious assumptions about the nature of offense. These assumptions can get you killed in another type of offense.

Unlimited offense means, quite simply, that *an individual is willing to do anything within his power to win—including violating the rules.*

Such a person is willing to resort to anything immediately available to keep from losing. As far as this person is concerned—at this moment—there aren't any rules. Anything goes.

This is why the football example in *The Last Boy Scout* is perfect. In a game of limited offense, one person shifted into unlimited mode. He used whatever means he had at hand to achieve a goal. The fact that he broke the conventions of limited offense is what is so shocking.

The main difference is that in a limited offense, there is awareness of other, long-term issues and repercussions—which determine limited rules of engagement. While winning is important, it isn't the only thing. When a situation goes unlimited, the individual doesn't care about anything but winning. At that moment, the long-term cost is irrelevant.

On a personal level people often say that in a *"real"* fight or a "street fight" there are no rules. This is not true; there are always appropriate levels of force, which define a direct response to the immediate threat. The question is, what kind of offense are you facing?

What endangers you is someone who shifts to unlimited offense. From there, you never know what you will be facing—except that it will be the nastiest thing he has immediately at hand. And when it comes to finding the nastiest thing possible, people are appallingly creative.

While unlimited offense is indeed the norm for certain circles, it is usually the last resort of those feeling overwhelmed and afraid of losing. This aspect is important because unlimited offense often is the result of starting to lose in what was initially a limited offensive situation. This is how a fight can escalate into a lethal-force conflict.

In other circumstances, two people using different systems can clash. One thinks in terms of limits while the other normally operates under unlimited offense. In these circumstances, the person using limited offense will most often lose. This is readily demonstrated when a civilian is attacked by a professional criminal. The sheer ferocity and degree of the assault overwhelms the victim.

This is what the proponents of so-called reality-based fighting mean when they say that there "are no rules in a street fight." Unfortunately, what they are advocating is that you, too, adapt the unlimited-offense mind-set. I say unfortunately because this mind-set breaks the rules of acceptable levels of force and is illegal. They are training to become the very monsters that they fear—as well as leaving themselves vulnerable to criminal and civil prosecution.

A broader example of unlimited offense would be terrorism. Terrorists use whatever is at hand to strike, and they are definitely not following any rules. However, like many people who operate within the parameters of unlimited offense, they rely on the other side to stay within the rules of limited offense.

Unlike limited offense escalating into unlimited offense, total offense starts out with no rules; its sole aim is annihilation. This isn't conquest, it is destruction.

On a personal level we are talking premeditated murder: cold, calculated assassination. This is most often seen in professional hits. On a cultural level we are talking genocide, whereby one group attempts to exterminate another. On a worldwide level it is the Cold War mentality of mutually assured destruction. If the button had been pressed, nobody on the entire planet would have survived.

Total offense is by far the rarest type, but it does happen. What is important is to realize that unlike unlimited offense—which is often based on an emotional or fear-based desire to keep from losing—total offense is the result of a conscious and "rational" decision to act.

Most people—even if they practice the martial arts—will never have firsthand experience beyond the most simple level of limited offense, at least in an amateur-sports context. They will spend time in the ring. This limited degree of experience will affect not only what they understand, but what they teach and, in turn, what their students will one day pass on to their own students.

It is critical to understand that in simple sports sparring, fence is a nonissue.

In fact, in most limited-offense circumstances, fence largely remains a nonissue. It isn't until you reach pro to semipro status in sports that strategies and tactics really become important.

There is no real need for fence at the amateur or recreational level. The nature of allowable offense under these circumstances is so constrained and circumscribed that the risk of serious injury is minimal (e.g., while it is possible to die in a touch football game, it is highly unlikely). You can "suck up" these offenses without serious injury. You step into the sparring ring expecting to get hit, not killed. Do not underestimate the impact that this will have on your strategies and priorities.

However, outside the sports context fence becomes a critical issue—especially when confronting unlimited or total offenses.

It is also critical to effectively achieve easy and quick victory in limited-offense situations, such as control tactics, or, just as often, in ending a fight instead of turning it into a drawn-out contest of strength and endurance—a situation that someone can easily escalate to one of unlimited offense.

The stakes go up in unlimited offense—as do the chances your opponent will inflict damage on you. To start with, you don't know if you are facing an unlimited-offense player or not. If he is the kind who will freak out and shift into unlimited, then you can't waste time and allow him to do so. You have to end it before he has the chance to upgrade to unlimited offense. And if what is coming at you is a total offense, you need to stay alive long enough to stop your attacker.

You must be concerned less with what you are going to do to him than with what he can do to you. As in the true art of *fence*, you have a three-foot straight razor, but so does he. This is no longer a case of your taking a few bumps and bruises when you lose. We're talking serious bodily injury if you don't understand fence.

In the amateur-sport way of thinking, there are only two basic categories: offense and defense. You are doing one or the other.

This is also where you get the popular understanding of comments like "the best defense is a good offense." The theory is your opponent is so busy defending, he doesn't have time to counterattack, much less initiate an effective offense.

One of the major stumbling blocks of mounting an effective offense is the belief that the other guy doesn't know the same things you do. He does, but he does them slightly differently. If you don't understand fence, it is going to turn into a contest of who can take the most punishment before giving up.

In my fighting days I loved people who felt that the best defense was a good offense. I could punish them all day long, all the while deflecting their attacks. They were so focused on their offense, they left themselves open. My counteroffensive not only ruined their offense, there was nothing to stop the damage I was inflicting.

Popular perception is that offense and defense are akin to a state line that you can simply cross to go from one to the other. You operate in one state or the other. Reality doesn't work that way.

To those without experience dealing with unlimited or total offense, going from defense to offense is like looking out across the desert. It looks flat and easy to race across to get where you want to go. But that is deceptive. There is a massive arroyo out there that will swallow your vehicle.

The wash that you can't see until it unexpectedly yawns open beneath your wheels is fence.

There is a chasm between offense and defense. If you don't know about it, you are going to fall in when you try to go from one to the other.

Offense   Fence   Defense

There are many analogies that I use to explain this concept. Pick the one that works for you. Fence is like twilight, a transitional period that has elements of both dawn and dusk; it is heading one way or the other, but is neither. Fence is like a military base in another country. It is the staging area for your offensive; a location from which you can effectively strike, yet which is protected and secure. The base's tactical location guards your homeland by presenting an immediate ability to apply force, while protecting your forces from enemy offense.

The analogy that works best for me, though, is of fence being like a bridge over the canyon that exists between defense and offense.

Don't just expect that bridge to be there. You have to build it across that chasm. That bridge is what will get your army (force) across. The bigger, better, stronger that bridge, the more troops you can get across and into offense. So, do you want to build a small, rickety, rope-and-plank bridge? Or would you rather build a suspension bridge where you can race tanks, Bradleys, and artillery across at 75 mph?

On top of everything else, with fence you now control the chasm . . . that air space is yours. If your opponent tries to build his own bridge, you can blow him to pieces. He is left with no option but to attack exactly where you want him to, i.e., launch an attack that you are set up and prepared to handle.

So that is the idea behind fence, but what is fence?

In its simplest form, *fence is putting yourself into a position where you can effectively attack your opponent, but he can't effectively attack you.*

Now think about what this gives you.

Your opponent is in your firing sights, but you are not in his. Your next move is an attack, while he will have to make a position change in order to attack you. Now the really bad news—for him, at least—is that you aren't going to let that happen. While he is trying to get back into position to attack, you are attacking effectively. If he ignores that attack, it's over for him.

Are you liking the sound of this? You should be.

What makes it complicated are all the different ways you can achieve this simple goal. Like driving a car, fence involves knowing how to combine basic elements to create the most effective response for the situation. If you take nothing else from this book, remember this: 90 percent of effective offense is building solid fence beforehand. When that happens, there is literally no difference between defense and offense. They flow together as one.

What components are needed to build a good fence? Turn the page . . .

— 3 —

The Three Components of Effective Power Delivery

Do you know the actual problem,
or are you just guessing?

—Tony J.

In the last chapter we talked about an advanced theory. The theory, while it sounds good, forces you to ask: How do I get there? The answer is by small, practical steps. In this chapter I want to introduce underlying concepts of the technical aspects of offense. As you acquire these simple, functional skills, developing fence becomes much, much easier.

In the first chapter I discussed driving, in order to show how the complex is a combination of the simple. In this chapter I want to introduce concepts that are the equivalent of braking, steering, and accelerating; in short, the basic elements of power generation and transference. This chapter will serve as a general introduction to them and an overview of ways to combine them. We will go into depth in following chapters.

Perhaps the most important aspect of the technical side of effective offense is this principle: *Your force goes where you want it to.*

The problems of putting your energy where you want it to go, however, are legion—not because it is necessarily hard to do, but because it is so easy to misplace.

Here's another "secret" about effective offense: Delivering force is less about what you do than about what you don't do.

That little shift in perspective lets you see all kinds of things you didn't before. It's not just about doing things that generate power, it's also about *not* doing things that rob you of power. The only reason delivering power is complicated is that *losing it is so much easier*.

When you know that, you start watching for actions that cause power loss.

But before we try to fix these problems, there's an important lesson in the chapter quote: Before you can fix a problem, you must understand what is involved—not what you think is involved, but what actually composes the problem.

If you don't understand the nature of the problem, your fixes won't work. In fact, they will contribute new levels and complexities to it. Instead of having one problem, you will have two or three.

I will tell you something that should have a major impact on how you think about offense. *Effective offense isn't about generating more energy, it is largely about losing less.*

Your natural body movement already generates sufficient force to get the job done. Your challenge isn't to generate more force. The trick is to determine how to apply what you already have to achieve the greatest effect. Anyone who has ever been dropped, stunned and in pain, to his knees by a wildly kicking child, thrown ball, or leaping dog can tell you that as small as these objects were, they had more than enough force to get the job done.

So, how do we find solutions to this problem? First, by identifying its nature. It is twofold. One aspect is loss of power; the other is putting power in the right place. Until you closely examine these as separate issues, it is very easy to believe they are the same.

In firefighting there is an older model called the Fire Triangle. Each side of the triangle represents an element—heat, fuel, and air—that must be present for a fire. Take away one of those elements and the triangle collapses. This simple model revolutionized firefighting strategies and technology because firemen no longer focused on fighting the fire, but instead destroyed the triangle that created the fire.

Effective offense can be described by the same triangle concept. There are three elements that must not only be present, but in the proper combination. Whether you lose power or it goes into the wrong place depends on which element of the triangle is missing.

For any empty-hand technique to be effective, you need three things.

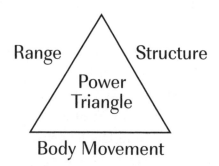

These components are to offense what steering, braking, and accelerating are to driving. Without any one of them, you are heading for a crash. And, as in driving, the challenge is learning how to combine them not only in theory, but in practice.

The analogy I use to explain the importance of these concepts is that of a farmer. Your field of crops (force) is your body movement. The market (target) where you are going to sell your crops is range. Structure (body pose) is the transportation required to get your crops to market. If you have all three, you have a winning combination. If one of these elements is missing, you will be unable to sell your crops (if you have any crops at all to sell).

Let's take a look at these one at a time.

Any technique has an optimum distance, the place where it is most effective. This describes range in its simplest sense.

Range involves knowing the distance within which the move will deliver the most force and placing yourself there.

If you are too close, there is a power drop. The same thing happens if you are too far. Range can also be destroyed by incorrect targeting, which we will discuss later. But know this now: You have to understand the effective range of any technique, and if you are not in that range, do not attempt it.

Let's talk about body movement. Before I discuss what I mean by this term, let's talk about what you think it means. Most people believe that power is generated from the hips. This is not necessarily true. It is, however, one of the most

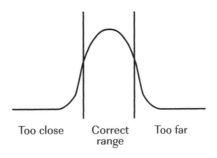

Too close Correct Too far
          range

common perceptions of body movement. Therefore, people try to generate force by turning their hips.

What few people realize is that moving into range is also body movement. In fact, *it is the main source of your power*. Additional body movements, such as hip twists, are not the source, but rather accelerators, of the power. They make what you have go that much faster.

This is a commonly misunderstood aspect of generating force and the basis of much confusion. If your body is moving forward at 10 mph, you don't arrest that action and then twist your hips to get your body moving at 10 mph again. This is exactly what most people do when they try to step forward, root, and then twist. Instead of flowing into a rooted position and accelerating that same momentum with a hip twist, they stop their momentum and then try to generate more.

If you are interested in hitting effectively, you first accelerate to 10 mph by stepping, and then, near the end of that move, accelerate an additional 10 mph by twisting. By doing it sequentially (i.e., stepping in and, before that movement stops, twisting) you have increased your body's movement to 20 mph. This is just one example of how to generate force through body movement. It also is one of the ways to achieve correct range.

It is misunderstanding both range and body movement that leads to one of the most common problems in losing power. In attempting to increase the power with a hip twist, many people inadvertently send a majority of that power shooting off in another direction, instead of into their opponents.

But until you sit down and specifically look for these problems, you will not notice them or their solutions. That's where the next few chapters will help you.

While the other two problems cause limited or misplaced power, incorrect structure will rob you of whatever power you have generated. This is why I said failure to effectively deliver power can be a twofold problem, of it not being present, or of it being lost.

If a foolish consistency is the hobgoblin of little minds, foolish structure is the hobgoblin of effective offense. This is how most power is lost. Structure when properly applied delivers all of the force generated by your body's movement. Structure when incorrectly applied is like trying to stab someone with a wet noodle.

Here's the rub. When I say techniques have certain ranges where they are the most effective, that also entails how you hold your body and limbs to deliver force at that range. If you do not pose and position yourself correctly, your body's natural tendency to bend and flex takes over. This puts in shock absorbers that rob you of power.[1]

If you are in the wrong range for a technique, any attempt to either compensate for it by adjusting your arms or deliver more force by using more muscle *will almost inevitably destroy your structure*.

This is why it is so utterly important to train to find the range of a technique. Not only must you be able to recognize the correct range for every technique you know, but you must be adept at stepping into that range. Training must be oriented toward teaching this concept. You cannot rely on its developing naturally with experience. Many students will never practice enough to really understand it—especially if you don't explain to them how to assess feedback.

---

1. Pose is how you hold your body to give yourself structure. Position is where you are relative to your opponent so that your structure can deliver force into him effectively. Positioning is an element of both range and structure.

I would also like to point out that I am not a large man. In fact, I am rather small and fine boned. While larger, stronger, and, yes, more aggressive people can often compensate for their lack of understanding through sheer mass, muscle, and aggression, a smaller person must compensate by having greater skill in applying these elements. If you do not apply a superior understanding, you will lose to a larger or more aggressive opponent.

So let's begin to look at these three elements one at a time. Each needs to be studied individually before you attempt to combine them. In learning their technical aspects, you will also learn how they apply to fence.

~ 4 ~

Understanding Range

Truth does not exist in isolation, nor is it proprietary. If something is "true," then you will be able to find manifestations and variations of it everywhere.

(Something I often say about martial arts politics)

There are three basic ways to get into range: one, you move into it; two, your opponent moves into it; or three, a combination of both occurs.

You will discover a similar situation with fence, except that formula would read, sometimes you move into position; sometimes you move your opponent into position; and sometimes both occur. I mention this because, as you will discover with proper practice, range and fence combine beautifully. Well, okay, beautifully for you; for your opponent, it sucks.

The defining element of range is knowledge of your goal. I don't mean a long-term goal. I mean an immediate one. What are you going to do in the next second? Your immediate goal is a critical component of reaching your long-term goal.

But until you start looking at these smaller goals, you won't see how important they are for reaching your bigger objective.

And you won't see how, if you don't meet them, you will never reach your bigger goal. If your immediate goal is to hit, then you have to make sure you are in the right range for the kind of blow you want to throw.

Of secondary, but only slightly less, importance is knowing your target. The proper target is instrumental in achieving the first goal. If you aren't in the right place, you are going to miss it. If you are too far back, you're going to give the guy time to move and you will miss that target.

If you hit a target, but your goal was something else, there is a good chance that you won't be able to exploit what happens. This is because you expected something different. You were aiming for his head, but you hit his arm. So what do you do now? This is a common problem because people often try to launch attacks from too far out, thereby giving the guy time to block.

Does this mean the attack failed? Not necessarily. There are many extremely nasty attacks you could apply against his arm. Unfortunately, most people are so focused on hitting the head that they can't "shift gears" fast enough to exploit new opportunities. This allows the opponent to withdraw his arm before the opportunity can be exploited. That means the whole dance has to start over again. So, in that case, yes, it is a failure.

It's a horribly common problem with most people's offenses. They are so focused on what they want to happen that they don't pay attention to doing what is necessary to make it happen. Put simply, they are so excited about "getting there" that they don't take the necessary steps. This is like being so excited about going on a trip that you forget to buy gas for your drive to the airport. Your plane is taking off, but you aren't on it; you are stranded on the side of the road.

Your attacks are more likely to "run out of gas" if you are in the wrong range. There are a lot of different reasons for this, but the easiest to explain is that your opponent will see it coming and do something to counter it. An attack thrown from the correct range is much harder to block or shed.

To keep this book at a reasonable size, I will discuss range only in the context of hitting (impact). However, many of the concepts we will discuss most definitely apply to other types of offense. For example, correct range is a cornerstone of effective takedowns and throws. If you are in the wrong range or position, you cannot effectively use your structure to destroy his. You will be trying to finagle muscle and speed to do the takedown for you. If his structure is intact, or if he is big enough, it simply won't work.

Let's talk first about targeting. Targeting with impacts (hits) is a horribly misunderstood idea.

In all types of offense, a very important concept is the vertical axis (VA). An axis is a line around which a body rotates. Like an airplane, human beings have three main axes.[1] While they can all be utilized in offense, the vertical is the easiest to manipulate and therefore the most useful.

In a standing position the vertical axis goes from the top of your head, through your body, out between your legs, and into the ground. This is the line on which your body will pivot when you are upright.

---

1. The three axes are vertical, front, and side. In aviation terms they control roll, pitch, and yaw. These control your bending, pivoting, and tilting. In a standing position you have one vertical axis running from your head through your body and into the ground. You have two horizontal axes. The front would be like a spear that enters beneath your belly button and comes out through your spine. On the same level a second line runs between one hip and the other. The point at which these three lines intersect is called your one point or center of gravity.

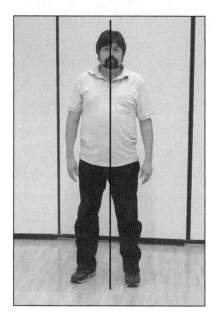 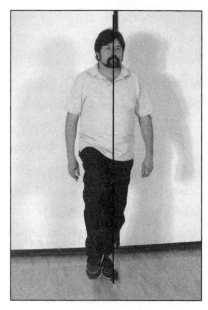

Body weight equally distributed
with VA in center.

Body weight over one leg with
VA through leg.

Your primary vertical axis doesn't move about within your body, but its exact location *moves with your body pose*. It is always in the center, where that center is always changing.[2]

Affecting and controlling someone's vertical axis is a critical component for both effective offense and creating fence. The possible ways to do this are nearly endless, and various styles achieve it differently. If you don't, however, you are not being effective and are wasting time—time that could cost you your life.

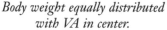

2. There is a slight complication here: although the primary vertical axis does not move with your chest cavity, the pose you take can and will a) twist your primary, b) create a new vertical axis, and c) determine whether it can be manipulated. For example, in a standing position the VA is the primary axis. On your hands and knees, however, the VA would be through your back somewhere around the bottom of your rib cage. In this position it would be extremely difficult to manipulate the new VA. In the same view certain twisty poses make it difficult to manipulate a person's mass around the primary axis. Two points arise from this one, even though the primary axis is not subject to easy manipulation, another has been created, too. The primary axis is still the target for an impact attack.

The VA's importance to impact attacks is that it is your target.
With an impact attack you try to "hit" the vertical axis. This is not controlling it, per se, but it does affect it. In order to strike the vertical axis with correct structure, you have to be in the proper range or position. Your arm is only so long. If you are too far away, it cannot reach. Your blow will fall short and not deliver power to the VA. The effective range of a move is a matter of inches. If you are too close, you won't be able to get up to speed on the move because you will be trying to push through his body instead of hitting. Both are losing propositions.

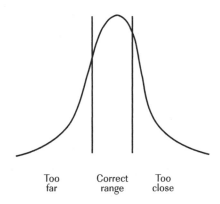

| Too | Correct | Too |
| far | range | close |

One of the main reasons why people don't understand range is that they don't understand the difference between a hit (impact) and a push (drive). When you shift your tactical thinking to include manipulation of the VA as a consistent goal, the difference becomes obvious. So does the significance and application of both impacts and drives.

A drive is any force that goes beyond the vertical axis. It is a push. Pushing is a very legitimate offensive tactic, but not when you are trying to hit.

With a drive your target is past the VA, and that is where you aim: through your opponent. Whether the drive is to move the VA from its current position or to spin the body around it depends on your goal (read: the technique you are using).

With an impact your target is the primary VA. No matter what its direction, your force is aimed at the VA. You want to think as though you could pass into his body, touch this "line," and withdraw. That is a hit, not a drive. This combination of both targeting and retraction ensures maximum force transfer into his body—not, as with a drive, through it.

Your target is where the force is delivered, so consciously choose it.

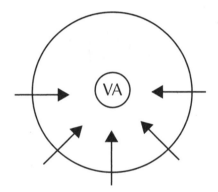

Incoming to VA.

In order to find the right range for a technique, you must be throwing it at the right target, the VA. No matter what direction your attack is coming from, you are aiming at his core. Your blow is like police sniper bullets, which are always aimed at the base of the brain. No matter what direction it comes in from, your attack is going to hit this target, the VA.

Failure to recognize the difference between a drive and an impact, combined with a lack of targeting, is why many people from sport-based arts have a hard time understanding range. It is also why they have such a difficult time delivering power into an opponent.

Range is a matter of mere inches. "Six inches past his back" and "the surface of his shirt" can be as much as a 2-foot difference! How can you find the effective range of a move if you are working with so much space? That's like trying to find a lost contact lens on a football field! Knowing that your target is the VA will help you find range much easier. With a fixed target, you will quickly discover what range you must be in to throw a blow with structure.

Let me give you a series of exercises to help you understand range a little better. You need to do this with every technique you commonly use. It also really helps to have a friend use a video camera while you are practicing. As an example, we'll use a right jab, right lead. You will need a heavy bag, boxing wraps (*not* gloves), and tape. My personal preference is a hanging bag because it gives you better feedback. Also, as you improve you will find yourself blasting over all but the heaviest and biggest floor-based strike trainers.

Start by placing a short piece of tape on the floor where the bag's VA would be (if you aren't sure, use a piece of string that stretches down to the floor when held in the middle of the bag's bottom). At 1-inch intervals, place additional pieces of tape in a straight line away from the first. Do this to a distance of about 3 feet. When you are finished, you should have a dotted line of tape spots leading to the bag's VA.

These dots are foot-placement markers. It doesn't matter if you use your toe, the ball, or the center of your foot. What does matter is that you put the same part of your foot on every "dot."

Have your friend hold the bag against his chest. Stand at the farthest point and throw a correct jab. Yes, you will be hitting nothing but air, but it is important that you do this to get the feel for correct form before you start making impacts. Jab, step, jab, step, advance to the next dot with every blow. With every jab, look closely at the distance to the bag's VA; not just its surface, but the bag's core.

As you get closer you will be tempted to lean forward or extend your arm out just a little, to reach. Don't. Stay in correct form. This is why a training partner who is watching you is important. He can see when you are sacrificing your structure in order to hit, and he can call you on it.

Your first jab that touches the bag should be a knuckle slap. As you move closer, your punches will start to feel stronger. Take careful note of this distance, both by "ranging" the bag and looking at your lead foot and which dot it is on. Have your friend tell you when the power feels strongest, when it grows, and when it diminishes.

Continue to move closer without modifying your blow. Don't try to hit harder or softer; try to hit with the same force. Don't adjust for range; just keep hitting the same way as you get closer and closer. You will notice that the closer you get, the weaker your punches become, until you aren't hitting at all, but just pushing the bag away.

The point where your punches are the strongest is the *correct range for that punch* and for your body type. Someone larger will have a different range, as will someone smaller. You will often find that even people of the same height will have different ranges because of different body types.

Now practice standing at the farthest point and stepping into the correct range. Learn to judge that distance. As you advance, don't look at the tape except to occasionally double-check yourself. Personally, I have students do this without hitting at first, but that is your choice. Add the punches at your discretion.

Once you teach yourself how far you have to step from the farthest point, start moving in, dot by dot, and stepping. The closer you get, the smaller the step needed to get into correct range, until your advance becomes a shuffle.

It is tempting while doing this to try to crank up the power and hit as hard as you can. I don't recommend this. My reasoning is that trying to hit hard distracts you from the real value of this exercise, which is to learn the range of this move. This is more of an intellectual exercise to learn a much misunderstood concept. Also, when you try to hit with power you will often lock down your muscles. In doing so you lose your sense of structure. Tight muscles blind you to the fact that you have lost correct structure and body positioning. That's why you need to have a friend watch you and tell you when you are losing structure. Besides, the real challenge is coming up next.

I have seen many boxers, muay Thai, and Krav Maga fighters skip into range, deliver a barrage of punches, then skip back and let the bag swing past them. This is a good strategy when you are in a limited-offense situation in which you don't need or use fence (e.g., a sparring match). However, this is a sport strategy. While it works very well in the ring, it utterly undermines the development of fence.

The next step is literally dancing with the bag. Your friend moves away. You step into correct range and jab the bag. It should move away from you slightly. When it does, you move forward into the new position and jab again. Every time the bag moves out of range, you reestablish range and jab again. Eventually, the bag will begin to swing back at you. Instead of leaping back, as many sports fighters do, I want you to move backward into range and fire off another jab. Your jab won't stop the bag's swing, only slow it down for a second. As the bag continues to move closer, you continue to retreat into correct range, jabbing as you go. When it starts moving away, close again.

By the way, be prepared for one hell of a workout doing this exercise. Even if you are in good shape, this continuous, machine-gun firing of punches is tiring. That's because people usually train for fast, three-hit spurts before retreating. That retreat gives them time to breathe and relax. Doing this exercise leaves no relaxation time. You are constantly hitting and moving. If you are used to two-minute rounds, don't be surprised if this wears you out in less than a minute.

Do this whole set of exercises with all the blows in your arsenal. With each move, you will discover there is a particular range in which it works best. Always remember that your target is the vertical axis of the bag. That is what you are trying to "touch."

When you have developed a good sense of the range for each and every blow you commonly use, begin to mix and match. Don't throw just one type, let the bag swing into range and fire off the most appropriate blow. You will find that by having ingrained the correct range for each blow, you won't have to think about what to throw next. The range will dictate the type of blow that you automatically fire. Don't worry about the bag spinning off into other angles, either. Learn to work them and skip out of the way.

A variation is to create other lines of dots starting at the farthest dot of your original line. Instead of coming straight in, cre-

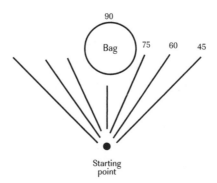

Triple Vs branching toward the bag.

ate a "triple V" pattern—that is to say, have not only a line coming straight in, but three Vs, one inside the other. One of the Vs is on the 45-degree angles, while the second is inside that, on the 60s, the third on 75s.

You will discover that if you follow one branch, you will still be able to do certain techniques. For example, a left jab still will be possible if you move a short distance down the left lines. By moving farther down those lines, however, you will not be able to effectively deliver power without first turning. While moving down the line will lend itself to a left jab, another line will lend itself to a cross. Don't try to force moves to work from different positions. There are moves that simply don't work from different positions. Knowing the information that this drill teaches is invaluable for understanding your next logical, and fastest move.[3]

At the beginning of the chapter, I said that there are three basic ways to get into range. One, you move into it. Two, your opponent moves into it. Or three, a combination of both occurs. These exercises teach you how to effectively do all three.

With time and with practice, you will find that you tend to gravitate toward where the bag's VA was originally. It is far easier to stand in the middle and slap the bag around you than to be chased around by it. I have worked out with many young, healthy fighters who, having exhausted themselves being chased around by the bag, stare in amazement at this little, middle-aged

---

3. I call this concept "graphing," which is how computer games often make decisions. It is a cognitive process for selecting the most effective response. If you have a field of twenty dots spaced an inch apart and were to draw inch-long lines between them, you could technically reach any dot from any other dot. To reach other dots, you would have to zigzag through other dots and connections. However, from any one dot there are certain immediate or optimal moves. These are your best and most logical choices. Unfortunately, a common strategic problem is that people don't do what is most effective from where they are; instead, they try to zigzag to a distant position. It is by knowing the range of your tools that you will greatly improve your ability to graph effectively.

guy—who is obviously in much worse shape than they—and who is casually dancing the bag three times as long as they do.

I can do it because I, who understand fence, am doing about a quarter of the amount of work that they are doing. I am literally hitting the bag where I want it to go for my next blow. But it takes a lot of practice to do that small amount of work while getting twice the results. More important, it takes a lot of thinking about what you are doing. A major component of that thinking is experimenting and finding out the importance of range.

As I said, range is critical for other types of offense. You can do a similar exercise with takedowns and throws. Have an uke take a stance so his VA is on one end of the dotted line. Your VA is on the other end. Proceed to work your way inward with a particular throw. You will find that there is a point where you can throw someone, but it requires muscle. The closer you get, the less muscle you use. However, get too close and you end up sacrificing your stability because you run into him.

— 5 —

Body Movement

In its relationship to strategy, logistics assumes the character of a dynamic force, without which the strategic conception is simply a paper plan.

—Cdr. C. Theo Vogelsang, U.S. Navy

Imagine a shipment of twenty-five crates that need to be delivered to a particular address by a certain date. The crates are of different sizes and weights. Because of these differences, the crates have to be shipped by different couriers and in a specific order to arrive at the same time. Let's further imagine that this shipment will "make" the company. Management has worked long and hard at setting up this deal and is just drooling over what is going to come from it—enough so that they are busy planning their next move and not paying attention to what is happening in the warehouse.

Now imagine that the guy doing the shipping is really sloppy and doesn't pay attention to what he is doing. Crates are shipped over a period of weeks, in no particular order. Worse, records are not being kept. On top of that, the guy is putting different addresses on the crates. And, just to make it a total nightmare, the guys calls in sick in the middle of it all. Everything is scattered, going everywhere except where it needs to go, and management doesn't have the faintest idea where anything is.

At the last minute, the VP of sales hears about this mess. He comes screaming into the warehouse and demands that everything be found and shipped out again, by an overnight courier . . . at 5:30 P.M. on a Friday. This creates a last-minute frenzy to put everything right again. But by then, it is far too late. The damage has been done. Things have left SNAFU and moved on to FUBAR.

Unfortunately, this corporate nightmare describes how most people try to create offense. That shipment is their body movement, those crates their power. Because they are so focused on what is going to happen after the shipment gets there, they aren't paying attention to what is happening in the warehouse. And that is where things start going wrong.

Power generation is about logistics. It's about coordination, so that things that move at different speeds all end up at the same place at the right time.

There is a mistaken assumption that if you do the technique, it will have power. Because of this, people do not focus enough on making sure that their moves meet code. Doing the technique does not automatically guarantee that you are generating or delivering power. Remember, a technique is a way to manifest principles. You have to make sure you are doing the things to generate power before you can deliver it through the technique.

With this background, a fundamental rule of effective offense will begin to make more sense: *You can't be so focused on attacking that you don't pay attention to what you are doing with your body.* That is like management making grand plans without being able to produce. First and foremost, you have to *manage your warehouse.*

If you don't, everything you plan will just be pie in the sky. Your logistics will be in total disarray. Your power will be scattered everywhere and totally off schedule. When that happens, your attacks will not have any power. You won't have what it takes to get the job done.

If people's training focused more on correct body movement and power delivery, their "fights" would be over in a quarter of the time. Here is an important safety tip: *Power, when correctly applied, will have an effect. The laws of physics guarantee it.* A move that lacks power and is misapplied won't have an effect.

Not to rain on anybody's parade, but if things aren't going well for you in a physical conflict, the odds are that the reason can be found in that tip. Putting it bluntly, the problem isn't with what he is doing as much as with what you aren't doing, and that usually boils down to bad logistics.

Without the logistics of proper body movement, all your strategy, all your techniques, and all your moves will be nothing but paper planning—paper that will blow away under the onslaught of his attack. That is how important the logistics of correct body movement are to your offensive efforts.

There are five fundamental aspects to effective body movement. These are the building codes that must be met in order to create and deliver force.

The first is moving into range.

The second is weight transference.

The third is eliminating extra (or nonproductive) movement.

The fourth is what I call "coherent movement," meaning that everything is moving in the right direction at the right time; in other words, logistics, making sure that what you need to get the job done is there when you need it.

Until your motion incorporates all four of the above, you aren't using your body properly. You are shipping crates all over the place, at different times and speeds. This means that you are creating all kinds of force, which goes everywhere—except where you want it to go.

When you can incorporate these four into every technique, then—*and only then*—can you move to the fifth element, acceleration.

Since I am BBQing sacred cows here, let me throw one more on the fire. Keep this one in mind at all times. If you forget it, you will open a Pandora's box of problems.

Acceleration is not the source of your power, it is an amplifier.

It is the finishing touch. It is the icing on the cake. It is the final polish. It is the dessert, not the meal. No matter how you say it, acceleration is not the meat of the matter. Unfortunately, too many people try to make speed the source of their power. They think of their attacks as bullets. They believe that the faster they go, the more deadly they are. Well, bad news here: no matter how you try, your hands and feet will never be as fast as a bullet.

Before you even think about putting speed into your moves, those first four elements must be in place. Why is this important? Simple: It doesn't matter how fast you get somewhere if it's the wrong place.

You may have all kinds of speed, but if those crates are being shipped to the wrong address, you're getting nowhere fast.

Having said all this about the importance of correct body movement, let me point out something about common methods of training. Proper body movement is not a *learn as you go* issue. It must be specifically addressed and drilled. While there will always be the "me, too" brigade of people claiming to have these fundamentals of body movement in their style/program/system, to put it bluntly, if this information isn't extensively covered and practiced, from the start, they don't have it.

There is another way that body movement is like logistics. Many people assume that they are experts—without ever having had any real experience of specific training. They assume that just because they know a style or system, by default they understand body movement and power transfer. Yeah, right. Let me put that attitude in other terms: Just because you shop at the supermarket doesn't mean that you can run the distribution network that it takes to stock those shelves. It takes some specific training, experience, and lots of skull sweat to make it all work. It takes even more to teach it.[1]

Body movement that *is* taught is commonly shown as part of something else, not as an individual component with many aspects. Therein lies a major source of confusion. Without isolating the different aspects of correct body movement, it is difficult to perfect any of them, much less combine them in effective movement.

A related point is that it isn't a matter of knowing about these issues. It's a matter of having them so ingrained that you instinctively use them in the middle of a fight. And that will only come through intensive training and practice to ingrain correct body movement into what you do.

With this in mind, I want you to realize that your body movement is the engine in the car of your technique. Without the engine, all you have is the outer shell. No matter how polished and spiffy it is, that chassis is useless as a means of transportation. That

---

1. In fact, how the body moves accounts for a large part of what is studied in certain disciplines—physiology, physical medicine, and their questionable cousin, kinesiology, to name a few. I have had some mind-numbing conversations about the nature of physical movement with people in these fields, as well as with doctors, coaches, and trainers from many different physical disciplines. The simplified version I am giving you here doesn't even begin to scratch the surface of these people's knowledge. There are Ph.D.s on this subject who freely admit that they know only a fraction of this topic. This subject isn't something you are going to master by going to the dojo twice a week for a few years.

also goes for your techniques. Without correct body movement, they're all form and no substance.

For ease of communication I will use *body movement* as an umbrella term that not only encompasses these different aspects, but is the sum of them, as well. We will identify and discuss each aspect individually, so you can recombine them into the greater whole of body movement.

Using the first four elements as a checklist, I can point out literally thousands of ways in which a good fighter uses effective body movement and an ineffective fighter doesn't—especially under the stress of live-fire situations. Without these four core elements of body movement, I guarantee, your offense will be undermined. You will rob yourself of power. What does arrive at the target will be too little to do the job.

I want to restate something here: *The subject of body movement must be specifically addressed, practiced, and understood before moving on to techniques.* It's not fun, exciting, or particularly easy. Above all, it doesn't look to students like martial arts. However, without an indepth exploration and practice of body movement before moving on to technique, body movement is exactly what will be unconsciously dropped under stress. If you want to survive a live-fire situation, these elements must be present.

As an example of what I mean by "specifically addressed and practiced," the first thing students entering my program are taught is how to shift their weight from one foot to another. The exercise is extremely simple. Put all of your weight over one leg, smoothly, easily, and without wobbling.

You then prove that your weight is correctly placed and that you are in balance by lifting your unweighted foot and moving it to different positions. Do this while keeping your arms down and without wobbling, pushing off to move your weight that last inch or so, without leaning, counterbalancing, or dancing the funky chicken to keep from falling over. Now stay there for a second before shifting your weight to the other foot.

That is all there is to it.

I should point out that I said this exercise is simple; I did not say it is easy. I regularly have black belts with as much as 25 years' experience in other styles wobbling like boiled eggs in an earthquake when they do this exercise because they have never individually focused on such a simple issue as weight transfer.

The object of the exercise is to be able to consistently shift your weight smoothly and easily so that all of it is over one leg. When you can do this without wobbling or adjusting, you are not only in balance and structured, but you can find this point without conscious thought. That means you can also do it under stress.

This is important because it is one of your strongest power generators. It is also critical for streamlining your movement, which is what makes you so much faster.

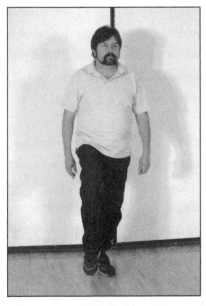 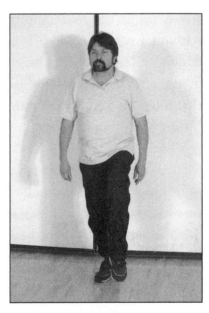

Weight over left foot (lift right leg).   *Weight over right foot (lift left leg).*

Do this exercise with a partner and watch for wiggles, wobbles, and little pushes to get into balance when you lift the light (unweighted) foot. This simple exercise will show you how well or how little the idea of body movement has been addressed in your training. You will be amazed at the improvement in speed, power, and performance that will result from just knowing where your weight is.

And that is what you learn from one simple exercise.

Let's take another look at moving into range, but from a different perspective. I have a trick question that I ask at seminars: What is the most dangerous part of a boxer?

Quite naturally, people identify his hands.

I tell them no, it's his feet.

His feet are what makes his hands dangerous. They carry him into the range to hit you. They take him out of the range of your blows. Most important, it is his feet carrying his body into range that gives his hands their power.

Without his foot movement, his hands are like that car without an engine. There is no power to make it go. Boxers are dangerous because they know how to fight from the bottoms of their feet. When their feet carry their bodies into range, that moving mass is what they hit with. In other words, they are hitting with momentum.

The foundation of any effective offense is momentum. *Movement is important, but correct movement is paramount.* Correct movement gives you momentum in one tight package. Those first four standards will help you create correct movement.

Momentum involves two elements, mass and velocity. In the physics formula, momentum equals mass times velocity. Velocity isn't just speed; it is speed plus direction. Again, it doesn't matter how fast you are going if you are heading in the wrong direction. That is why speeding things up when they are going every which way doesn't work.

Furthermore, creating momentum is a matter not only of how fast one part moves, but of *everything* (i.e., your mass) moving in the same direction.

The more you have moving in the same direction, the less important speed is. A freight train might not move very fast, but it will make a hash out of anything that gets in its way. Keep this idea of a freight train moving down the tracks because it will help you understand coherent movement.

Your mass in motion is your payload. What many people fail to realize is that the simple act of stepping into range is your freight train. You have generated all kinds of momentum with a simple step. It is at this point, unfortunately, that many people destroy their momentum by first stopping their momentum, then trying to get more power by either speeding up or twisting. That's where the mistakes that rob them of power start, but we'll get to that in a bit.

A close cousin of stepping into range is weight transfer. This is a poorly understood concept and is often mistaken for stepping. A step is not the same as weight transfer. While you can't really step without transferring your weight while walking, you can transfer your weight without stepping. The previous exercise just had you doing it. If you are not walking, it is possible to step without transferring your weight.

This lack of distinction leads to a lack of understanding. With that comes the destruction not only of timing, but of coherent body movement. That is because in most moves the source of power is based not on the step, *but on the weight transfer.*

Let me give you the most basic example: I have seen people taught to hit "on the step," so that blow and foot land at the same time. I have also seen people taught to step, twist the hip, and then hit. So which formula is right? Both and neither. Both work for specific situations, both fail in others. Trying to use either as an always-do-it-this-way rule is setting yourself up for failure at least half of the time. Much of the time, however, I see when people attempt to do what they think will generate power, they end up doing a screwed-up combination of both that scatters their momentum to the four corners of the room. This is because they are moving in multiple directions and/or their timing is way off. Most of the time it's an inefficient combination of both.

Simply stated, *the hit or attack occurs with the weight transfer.*

That little statement not only encompasses both theories on hitting, but explains the potential problems with both examples. It also describes the most common timing issues.

Since you want to hit someone with your momentum (moving body weight), it doesn't matter whether your foot lands first or you hit as your foot lands. Both are valid timing—if you focus on hitting on the weight transfer. You can shift your weight as you put your foot out just as effectively as you can put your foot out and then shift your weight.

Problems happen if you hit before or after the weight transfer. If you hit before, at best what you are doing will turn into a glorified push. In that case your moving body weight will turn your punch into a drive. This is a perfectly valid and useful technique, if that is what you mean to do. This, however, assumes that you don't goof and retract, as you are supposed to do with an impact. If you do that, while your body weight goes forward your delivery system (arm/leg) is retreating. There is no delivery of force when that happens.

If you hit after the weight transfer, you strike with nothing but the muscles of your arm or the weight of your leg. In combination

Punch and step at same time (drop step hit): neutral.

Step and hit at same time.

Moving foot first: neutral.

Foot placed.

Weight transfer and hit.

with correct range and structure, this can be a useful way to coun-terattack a charging opponent. But if incorrectly done, it turns into a mushy pushing action that resembles an attempt to shove off your opponent.

Go to the bag and try these different timings with a simple jab. Five minutes of hitting on the weight transfer with this one punch will go miles to clarify what I am talking about. This also has serious implications about timing and communicating to your students what is wrong with their techniques.

Many people make a mistake in that they move their weight, pause, and then try to generate force from their hips. This arrests their momentum, which they try to make up for through a hip twist. That twist is not the source of power, but an acceleration and channeling of the momentum you already have; momentum you acquired when you trans-ferred your weight.

Just as common are fighters who automatically twist their hips as they step. This creates a physics that sends a signifi-cant portion of their momentum off on another line, instead of where they want it to go. By twisting too much, they throw their weight in the direction they are twisting—not into their opponent.

While there are times to do a weight transfer and hip twist simultaneously, for most blows you should wait until near the end of the transfer before twisting the hips. By waiting you will not overdo the hip twist, which is a common result when some-one believes that the hip twist is the source of power. They overcommit to try to get more power. In doing so, they lose power.

The reason this problem is not commonly recognized is that sports fighters can sacrifice their structure in order to get the hit. In a sports context, the point is still awarded because the blow still lands. By twisting out of correct position and changing direction, they don't deliver power, but they still make contact. If the blow's direction was not modified in order to hit, it would be obvious where the excessive hip twist takes the power—as can be seen by what happens to the straight punch illustrated below.

Without hands-on instruction, it is difficult to teach all the subtleties of weight transfer. What I can say is that the timing for striking with weight transfer is near the end. This also goes for kicking.

In both timings, wait until your body is moving before launching the blow. There are several reasons for this. Waiting until near the end before moving your limb gives your body weight time to pick up speed. This timing is also important because your limbs are faster than the rest of your body; although they start later, they arrive at the same time as your weight transfer ends.

Neutral, hands raised with right coming out in punch.

Step/weight transfer/excessive hip twist.

Blow heading off to 45.

Another point is that by waiting until your mass is moving toward the target, you have increased your chances of the blow's landing because there is less time for your opponent to block or move. All he sees is you moving; the blow doesn't materialize until you are in range. By moving into range you have not only positioned yourself to deliver force, but have created a freight train to carry it to where you want it to go.

If you are working on takedowns, you can practice weight transfer in two ways. One is by creating a structure that *enslaves* your opponent to the weight transfer. This means you set up range, structure, and direction. As you transfer your weight, you drive or pull him where you want him to go. Since he is locked to you by structure, you are moving him from the beginning of your weight transfer.

I should point out that seldom will this move alone cause him to fall over. By simply putting your foot next to his and dragging or knocking him over your foot, you can often get a swift takedown. I would point out, however, that doing this action before pivoting 180 degrees and dropping your center makes takedowns or throws work far better than if you just do a turn and drop.

Another way of doing this is by determining direction and range before moving. You wait until near the end of the weight transfer before putting in structure. You "bump" your opponent with your structure or knock him into your moving structure, either of which destroys his structure or balance and allows him to be taken down.

These kinds of moves work best with either a trip (knocking him over a previously placed foot); a downward pull as you are impacting (e.g., having gripped his wrist, you pull it down as you bump); or, even better, a combination of both. Specific angula-

Extended limb, weight forward.

Weight transfer, with limb still extended.

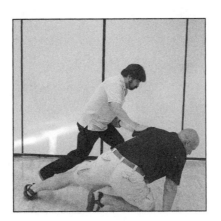

Dragging him over by turning and lowering center.

tions work best and greatly reduce the amount of force you need to use.[2] However, failing that, you can often get away with pulling hard to create a teetering effect and then knocking him over.

In each case you connect your opponent to your weight transfer. The matter you must focus on is *when* to do it. Failing

---

2. For anyone interested in learning these specific angulations, I would heartily recommend seminars with either guru Steve Plinck or Tristan Sutrisno. Both are masters of angulation and positional fighting.

Extended limb weight back (other hand held).

Weight transfer pull, fold back forearm.

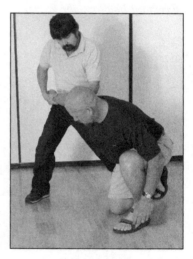

Transfer weight so elbow (structure) strikes.

Slave him again.

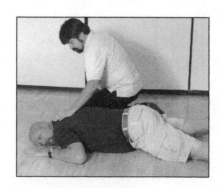

Put him down.

to differentiate between these two timings is the root of a lot of problems that beginning students have with their throws.

In any type of offense, you must be careful not to collapse your structure during the weight transfer, thereby allowing your limb to fold up in one direction while moving in another. This commonly takes the form of a person moving forward while his or her arm collapses. Then, after the weight transfer, the person attempts to push or pull using muscle and a rooted stance.

This common mistake is most often seen with smaller people who try to muscle larger practice partners. Larger people do it too, but their size and strength often allow them to succeed in using muscle in this way against a smaller opponent.

I would like you now to go back to the heavy bag with your dots. Do all your preferred moves and practice hitting near the end of the weight transfer. Use the ranges you already know for the various techniques. Try it both ways. Sneak your foot into position and then shift your weight. Then try stepping first and,

Extended limb weight back.

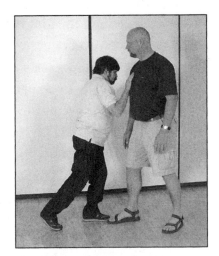

Transfer weight forward, collapsing limb "coiling up."

at the last minute, shooting your strike out, so that your strike and foot land at the same time. With both methods, the trick is to practice starting your hit near the end of the weight transfer and your retraction when the weight transfer is completed. The time for the blow to snake out and come back is often much shorter than you may have thought.

You will discover many things by doing this, so many that I can't begin to tell you about them all. What I can tell you is that the more you look, the more you will find. Often, things that have never before made sense will "click."

Knowing the other four fundamentals will greatly assist you in avoiding extra (or unproductive) movement. This avoidance is the third fundamental of effective body movement.

Extra movement largely comes from an attempt to generate more force; for example, cocking back to throw a harder punch. The truth is that such an attempt not only leaves the puncher exposed to a counterattack, but doubles the time of his attack. This makes it more likely that he will be counterattacked through the hole he created. That's just one problem. Another is that even though the idea is to hit harder by having picked up more speed, you don't get somewhere faster by going backward before going forward.

All of this leads to something else: Extra movement tends to ensure that you are not in the right place for timing, range, position, or structure. The reason is that instead of moving just a few inches from where you were, you go all over and then have to come back and try to find the right place. By putting in extra motion, you've made the area you have to search to find the right position one of feet rather than inches. Now, because of all the wasted effort, you have less time to find the right spot. More area to cover and less time to find the right spot is not a winning strategy.

I explain this concept by saying that it takes one second for an effective blow to travel the distance and hit. It takes a second, however, for it to cock back, then another second to return to its starting position. From there it still takes one more second to travel the original distance. So now, instead of taking one second, your punch takes three seconds because you decided to run around the track to hit "oh, so much harder."

There is another reason to eliminate extra or unproductive movement. Even if he doesn't counterattack, such movement tells your opponent what is coming. If he has time to see it coming, there is a good chance he will be able to do something to foil it. You have to learn how not to warn your opponent of what you are about to do. As the old saw goes, "forewarned is forearmed"—even if the forearming is nothing more than bracing for impact by tightening muscles.

Don't try to make your moves more powerful by adding extra movement. To do so reflects an amateur attitude that causes more trouble than it is worth. To recognize whether you are doing this, either have a friend watch you or videotape yourself working out. You will be amazed at how much extra movement you can edit from your techniques by watching for it.

Coherent motion is based on awareness of moving your body. How you do it largely depends on your style and its origins. Eastern and Western fighting styles have significantly distinct means of generating force through different types of body movement.

There are some incredibly sophisticated and powerful methods in both Eastern and Western fighting styles. These methods may be sneered at as "wrong" by practitioners of a particular discipline, but by moving his body in that "wrong" way, a practitioner of a differing style can hit you hard enough to get you a speeding ticket in El Paso.

The reality is that there are many *"right"* ways to do things. This causes confusion among people who want only one Right™ way to do things. I have lost count of all the different ways I have had my chimes rung, but, let me assure you, they all delivered power. How you move is a matter of personal and stylistic preference. If you aren't comfortable with how a style moves, try another style.

Let me give you the most basic example of coherent body movement: moving from your center, rather than from your head and shoulders. Once you have this awareness you can begin to play with it and discover different ways to move your body to generate force. But without this fundamental awareness of coherence, your attempts to generate power through body movement will result in your crates being shipped all over the place at different times.

I refer to the way that most people walk as a "rock fall." Using geology as the example, a boulder gives way. As it rolls downhill, it knocks loose other rocks. Their combined movement builds incrementally and creates a rock fall. Way below where the first rock came loose, a cascade of rocks and debris comes crashing down.

For some people their head is the original boulder. They lean their head, which pulls their shoulders forward, thus starting a rock fall. That fall drags the rest of their body along. Then they put a foot out and catch themselves from falling. Mind you, they don't arrest their forward motion; their foot placement just keeps them from falling down. They keep leaning forward and continue their forward movement, dragging the rest of their body along and catching themselves before falling. This is how they walk. In fact, they control their forward speed by how far forward they lean.

You can see what I mean by walking across a large area and continually "pecking" like a chicken with your head and shoulders. You will find that you can increase and decrease your speed by how far you lean forward or backward.

While the example I just gave is an extreme exaggeration, you will find that a less extreme version describes how most untrained people move. Most people walk from their chest, not from their "center." I used the head because it is the most obvious example. Once you recognize movement from the head, you will be able to locate the same mode of locomotion stemming from the chest.

I am not saying that this is the wrong way to move. In fact, it works wonderfully for walking. What I am saying is that moving this way in order to generate power is not coherent.

It is, in fact, towing the rest of your body along and then running to catch up. As anyone who has ever pulled anything using a rope knows, there is a split second before the slack is taken up. During that moment, there is now power transfer. Once the slack is taken up, the object that is being pulled begins to move.

In an offensive situation, you don't want that down time.

A rock fall starts from the top, but an avalanche begins in the middle of what slides. Let's use a snow avalanche as compared to a rock fall to explain coherent movement. With an avalanche, a new layer of snow piles on top of an iced-over, older layer. The weight of the new snow pushes the new snow off the ice. In other words, it slips. When that happens, everything moves. It both pushes against what is below and drags along and frees anything above. If you watch an avalanche, you see the entire side of a mountain begin to move at once.

Basic coherent motion is like this avalanche, not like a rock fall. Your entire mass is involved from the start. It doesn't start small and get bigger. It starts big and just gets bigger as you accelerate. In its simplest form, coherent motion means learning to move your hips and shoulders forward at the same time. Everything *slips* at once.

Your torso literally slides off your legs. It doesn't tip; it is pushed forward. And it is pushed off the top of your legs. As such, your entire trunk moves forward simultaneously.

You can understand the difference by taking any object that is taller than it is wide and setting it at the edge of a table. First, putting your hand near the top, push the object gently and tip it over. Have your other hand about an inch lower than the pushing hand, on the other side of the falling item. As it tips over, catch it. This is how most people normally "walk." Now push the object gently off the table from somewhere near its base. Do this so that the object doesn't tip over, but instead drops into your waiting hand. Again position your other hand about an inch lower and on the side of the object and catch it from underneath when it falls. Pay very close attention to what it feels like when you catch it each time.

If you do this a few times you will discover that while the same amount of energy is delivered to the object in both circumstances, in the first, the object topples gradually; it doesn't land in your hand all at once. In the second circumstance, the object drops into your hand all at once, no matter how gently you push it off.[3]

This exercise of knocking something off a table illustrates the differences in force between the two ways of moving and how they deliver power, either drawn out over time or all at once.

Knowing this, you will now understand when I say that many people attempt to generate an attack using a walking body motion. It is during the time lag between the chest mov-

---

3. One of the defining characteristics of impact is the time it takes for force to be delivered. The shorter the time, the greater the impact. To this end, air bags don't lessen the forces involved in an accident, but stretch the time and slow you down before you hit the steering wheel. This is also why you retract from an impact. Such an action shortens the time of impact.

ing and the hips following that their offense starts to fall apart. They have lost their coherence of movement. They move like a rock fall instead of an avalanche.

Returning to the analogy of business and shipping, in terms of generating force, the shipment trickles in, instead of being delivered all at once. Now think in terms of customer satisfaction. If the shipment turns into a total fiasco, the customer will cancel the order. The same goes for your opponent, but instead of canceling the order, he will dodge delivery. The second he feels your first touch, he's going to move or counter. This is happening while the rest of your shipment is somewhere out there in transit. By the time the rest of the shipment gets there, he's gone.

If you take nothing else from this chapter, remember this: Your opponent is not going to stand there and wait for you to get your act together. When you start to think about it in this manner, you will begin to see why so many offenses fail.

An offense that uses coherent body movement—with correct range and structure—puts everything into him at once. The shipment arrives intact, all at once, and right where you want it to go, giving him no chance to cancel the order.

In the appendix I give a more detailed version of one of my favorite forms of coherent body movement. It is a method I have found very useful for Westerners and people who don't have much time to train.

Recognizing the importance of the first four aspects of effective body movement is your best chance to avoid trying to fix the problem of power loss with speed. Before you even think of adding speed, make sure you have the elements of moving into range, transferring weight, eliminating extra or unnecessary movement, and coherent body movement firmly under your belt.

Not only does trying to fix power loss with speed not address the real problems, but it makes you more likely to go zipping past the place where you have to be in order to have structure. That just adds to your existing set of problems.

Having said that, however, acceleration—when properly applied—makes something that is already big and nasty, bigger and nastier. Used correctly, acceleration is like a missile. It comes at your opponent entirely too quickly for his comfort . . . and, hopefully, faster than he can do anything about.

But aim your missile first.

All of your work to meet the first four essentials of correct body movement amounts to aiming that missile so that it has the shortest and most direct flight. It is like the submarine that surfaces just offshore and then fires a missile. From that range there really isn't much of a chance for either (a) the missile to miss or (b) your opponent to keep the missile from hitting.

It is important to recognize the timing of this maneuver. As with the submarine, a lot of prior work went into making the flight time of your attack (missile) so short.

Many people make a mistake in offense by launching their missiles too soon and from too far away. They are in such a hurry to fire off an attack that they haven't done their logistics or put themselves properly in place. In the submarine analogy, they try to fire their missile while coming out of their own port, and they do this without exact coordinates for their target. The problem is that the missile they just launched is short-ranged. The odds are that it doesn't even have enough fuel to get where it needs to go.

Putting aside the analogy, many people start moving their hands at the same time they start moving their bodies. Unless they are coming from a long distance, this is a mistake. Their limbs move faster than their bodies, so their attacks reach their targets before they have built up momentum. By the time their moving bodies have created momentum, their attacking limbs are already on the way back. Therefore, their attacks have no payload to deliver.

A general rule of thumb—and something you need to experiment with to find the timing—is that in any attack, in close proximity and with your hands in front of you, your body moves first, and then you launch the attack as you are entering range. The same tends to apply to attacks coming from your rear limb. Your body's movement and weight transfer either pushes or pulls your limb.

There are exceptions to this. One is when you have perfected (or practiced a system that uses) subtle body movements. A player of these systems can extend a limb first and then, with a fast, subtle "wiggle," put his entire body weight and movement behind the move. Another exception is a person who puts structure out in front of him and then with his body movement clears a pathway to enter (kind of like a snowplow clearing the way with its blade).

This last approach is not a sports strategy. It is more suited for effective resolution of conflict. Although you can practice doing it in the ring, it is not guaranteed to bring you victory in point sparring.

There is a significant difference between strategies. In a sports match you will often see people who drive in and then pull back. A person pushes in, attacks, and then does a weight transfer back in order to fire off either a point-scoring blow or a counterstrike to keep his opponent from following him as he retreats. Often, at that point, the person steps back out of range. In the ring people are always hopping in and out of range. They attack, back off, attack, back off. Speed and endurance are critical in this ongoing situation.

In effective offense, however, you enter into range and continue to press attacks. By this I don't mean that you do the same attack over and over again, but that you begin to unload a plethora of attacks that are appropriate for that range. You use a variety of attacks that are not limited to impacts. If you shift your weight back, that, too, is an attack because you are pulling your opponent with you in order to knock him off balance, break his structure, throw him, or, having grabbled a part of him, draw him toward you.

By recognizing this fundamental difference in strategy, you will not only see the difference between sports fighting and actual conflict, but also how an overemphasis on speed will undermine your offense's effectiveness. That's because you are going so fast you don't take the time to make sure you have all the necessary components.

When you are in range and your body is moving, you have power. It is at that time that you snap your structured limb out, not only to deliver the blow, but to increase your velocity. You wait until the last minute to speed things along.

Acceleration is a drag race, not the Indy 500. You only have to go a quarter-mile, and in one direction. But everything else you have done has put that dragster into position to go speeding down the strip.

It is that last-minute burst of speed that makes what is already an ugly monster even uglier. What was coming at your opponent at 20 mph is suddenly traveling at 120.

You will find that waiting until the last minute before accelerating (launching your attack) greatly increases your chances of success. Your attacks will be blocked far less often. Now, instead of waving your hand in the air from way back and saying, "Yoohoo! I'm attacking now!" your attacks will be more like the submarine suddenly surfacing and launching missiles. In other words, it's very hard for your enemy to keep from getting nuked.

～ 6 ～

Structure

Amateurs talk about tactics, but professionals study logistics.

—General Robert H. Barrow, Commandant,
U.S. Marine Corps

If someone were to terribly violate the rules of range, it would be easy to see. Either the blow would miss entirely or the person being struck would be pushed backward. With body movement, violating the rules would also be obvious. Either the striker would not move at all, or his body would veer off in a direction other than where he wanted his force to go.

The reason most people don't see violations of the rules of structure is that they tend to happen too fast.

Imagine a car crash test. These are filmed at extreme slow motion so that engineers can watch the physics of a crash. With slow-mo, every bend, wrinkle, and fold of a crash is closely watched and analyzed. Design improvements to resolve problems are made from this analysis.

The same could be said of flaws of structure. We can see the results—or lack thereof—but the details often occur too quickly to see. They happen within the time of a punch—or, to be more specific, within the time of impact. That isn't a long time in which to see the problem. Because it all occurs so fast, we don't realize the significance of structure or how poor structure robs us of power.

Structure is, in its simplest sense, the use of your skeleton, tendons, and muscles to both deliver and resist force.

But—and this is where it can get tricky—*it also involves executing a move in such a way that you remove "shock absorbers."*

In case you hadn't noticed, your limbs bend. If your limbs bend when you don't want them to, they become shock absorbers. Without proper structure you're hitting with a foam tube that bends and flexes, instead of a club. You hit as hard as you can, but, because of the flexibility of the foam tube, the energy is not transferred. The trick is to get your limbs to bend when you want them to and not to bend when you don't want them to.

While this whole bending-limb idea may seem obvious, the odds are against your getting it correct if you don't specifically look into the mechanics.

Because structure is closely related to range, a poor understanding of the latter will greatly complicate your task of understanding structure. For example, if you are in the wrong range and you still try to make the hit, you will sacrifice structure. To gain that extra distance, you have to move out of the correct structural position. For the sake of those extra inches, you are now hitting with a foam tube instead of a club.

When examined in the context of range, the idea of structure should cause all kinds of lightbulbs to go on in your head. You will be able to clearly identify problems that have plagued your attempts at offense. It will help you fix your tools. No longer will you be trying to *drive nails with a broken hammer*.

The truth is that structure—and the importance of creating correct structure—is a massive topic, worthy of its own book.

Structure affects everything from balance, correct movement, timing, grounding, effective power transfer, and countless other issues of both offense and defense. The more you look into it, the more important you will realize it is. For the sake of brevity I am going to describe structure in a punching context, since this is how most people are trained in offensive skills. It will serve as a familiar way to introduce this topic, but structure is also critical in other types of offense.

The easiest way to explain the importance of structure is to imagine trying to quickly punch someone with a big spring. The harder you try to hit, the more energy goes into the spring.

This is what I am talking about when I say incorrect structure robs you of power. Unfortunately, the way most people try to strike is as if their entire arm were one giant shock absorber. When they hit, their arm coils up. To be more accurate, at the moment of impact their limbs either flex or collapse entirely at wrist, elbow, and shoulder. This spring effect is lost in the withdrawal of the punch.

When you deliver force, you also receive it. This is a basic law of physics: For every action there is an equal and opposite reaction. You're not only putting force into something, but equal force is coming back at you. That, combined with the fact that our limbs bend, creates shock absorbers.

I must beg your indulgence for a quick side trip into physics and physiology. If you were to dive off the bow of a small boat, the force of your forward dive would push the boat backward. Your forward movement pushes the boat back at the same time because of the equal-and-opposite law of physics.

I use this example because it shows this force clearly, whereas walking doesn't. When we walk, the same force that would push the boat back is being pushed down and back into the earth. But in case you haven't noticed, the earth is bigger than you, so it isn't likely to be pushed backward when you walk. Because of the earth's refusal to yield its right of way to our walking, very few people notice the dynamics of force. All they see is the forward motion.

The second reason we seldom notice how force works is because of the structure, which allows this energy transfer in the most efficient way. An overwhelming majority of the force is handled not by muscle, but by the alignment of your leg and hip bones. The reason walking isn't hard work is because your skeleton takes the brunt of the force; it is being channeled into the strongest alignment possible.

For an example of alignment, place one end of a kali stick against a tree and, holding the other end, push straight in. You will end up stalling there. Your forward force will not break the stick because of the alignment of the fibers within the stick. If, however, you were to hold the stick sideways, grasping each end, and then press against the tree with the middle, the odds are that the stick would break and it would break under less force than you were applying previously. In the case of the broken stick, the pressure was not coming from a direction in which the fibers were aligned to resist it. Bones can easily break as a result of force coming in sideways, but they seldom break if it comes from the direction that they are designed to take it. If the latter were the case, we wouldn't be able to walk without breaking our legs.[1] This illustrates the importance of structural alignment.

The combination of structure and the earth's not moving away as we walk is why we seldom think about force as a

---

1. While it is possible to shatter your limbs in the direction they are designed to take pressure, the amount of force must be tremendous, e.g., the equivalent of jumping off a five-story building.

two-way street. Nature has designed us so our bodies can easily handle these forces under normal operating conditions.

Unfortunately, offense is not a normal operating condition. As such, Mother Nature doesn't do all our homework for us. We have to consciously consider—and control—alignment structure, and how we hold our bodies (pose). In other words, we have structure only if we intentionally align our bodies correctly.

Let me point out that there are structural postures that allow our bodies to align to handle force. When we are in these poses, both the generation and reception of force seems nearly effortless . . . or at least far less difficult. Because your structure absorbs it, you don't really feel the amount of force being applied or received.

Amazingly enough, this is often misinterpreted by people who don't think they did anything because it didn't feel like hard work. People often *will train themselves to hit incorrectly because it feels as if they are hitting harder when they don't have structure.*

They feel they are hitting harder because their muscles, not their structure, take the brunt of the force. It's like breaking the kali stick: there is actually less force—although more spectacular results—than if you were to press against its structure.

In truth, their hits are weaker because they haven't aligned their structure to handle force. Under the equal-and-opposite-force law, their limbs collapse until they reach one of these *structural poses* that can both generate and receive force. Even though their sensory feedback is saying, "Wow, great hit," they are, in essence, hitting their opponent with a shock absorber.

Unfortunately, by that time three major problems have arisen. One, that particular offense is nearly over. Two, a majority of the initial force already has been lost. Three, your opponent is probably countering by now.

So what are structural poses? Think about pushing a car. There are two main positions that people tend to take. In one, the head is lower to the ground than normal, one foot is back, and the arms are fully extended and locked straight in front. This pose tends to occur when the car is already rolling or several people are involved. In another position, the body is much lower to the ground, one foot is back, and the other foot much closer to the car, the elbows are down, and the hands are nearly tucked into the armpits (or, if you will, the thumbs are looped in the suspenders). This second pose tends to be used to start the car rolling, especially when doing it alone. In both cases the body is held diagonally in order to push along a horizontal plane. Both poses allow effective power transfer.[2] They are structural postures that allow us to *lock down* our structure in order to deliver force.

Young or inexperienced people will often try to push a car with their arms either not fully extended or collapsed. They will start with their arms bent, their elbows horizontal to the ground. You will see someone attempting to push a car this way either extend out or collapse into one of the two structural positions I just described.

Their muscles alone cannot withstand the force they are generating when they are not in a structural pose. *When you cannot withstand the force you are generating, you cannot transfer that force into your opponent.* That energy is being bled away into your shock absorbers (e.g., your elbows bending).

I mentioned earlier that auto accidents are filmed in extreme slow motion because the crash happens too fast to see. Watching

---

2. The third option is to turn your back to the car and put your hips against the trunk. This allows you to use the structure of your legs to deliver force without the possible shock absorbers of your torso and arms. It is, in fact, the easiest way to get the car moving at first, then switch to either of the other two positions.

someone attempt to push a car incorrectly is the same process as a structural collapse during an offense, but slowed down so that you can see what is happening. The reason you can see it with a car is that it is a long, drawn-out process. An offense happens too quickly to be easily seen.

Let's go back to our simple punch. How long does it last? For ease of explanation, let's hypothetically say that the impact itself lasts one second. But the thrust, impact, and retraction takes three seconds, one second for each. This exaggerated model gives us a bigger, slower picture. Now, assuming that you have synchronized range, structure, and body movement, the power delivery would look something like this.

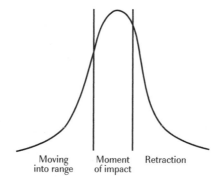

Moving into range   Moment of impact   Retraction

Even though the whole process lasts three seconds, the power is delivered in one concise package and all in the same moment. That is how it should be.

Unfortunately, many people are not in a structural pose when they strike. This means that while there is an initial impact, the limb collapses against the resistance until it reaches a structural pose. A majority of the force is absorbed by the collapse only. If they continue to press the same attack in the form of a drive, there will be a secondary power spike, where force would be delivered effectively.

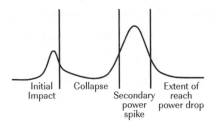

But this happens only if they continue to press forward. Here is where the idea of trying to punch six inches past someone suddenly begins to make sense, although it is a lazy way to compensate for bad structure. Somewhere along the process of his arm collapsing, the person will find structure and the second spike will occur.

The problem with that idea, however, is that the move is no longer an impact, but rather a drive. A drive is a legitimate offense, as anyone who has ever had his legs cut out from under him by a muay Thai kick can tell you. Impacts are supposed to retract before they become pushes. While a drive does have impact qualities, its goal is to push through an object. It does this by not retracting.

The reality is, however, that by the time the second power spike occurs, most people would be retracting. Remember, the punch only lasts one second. Punches that are not delivered in a structural position would look something like this.

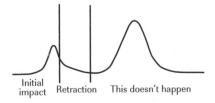

It is not that the power isn't there. It is lost through the structural collapse instead of being effectively delivered. To deliver force this way, you need four seconds, with the third second spent continuing to press the attack before retracting.

I cannot tell you how many times I have seen structural collapse rob people of power and extend the duration of a fight. If you have ever seen someone "take a punch" that should have floored him, the odds are that you have seen structural collapse, too. I would conservatively estimate that 90 percent of the time it wasn't about how the tough guy could take a punch. It was a matter of poor range and structural collapse on the part of the hitter. A lot of tough guys who pride themselves on their ability to take a punch change their tune when hit by someone who knows how to do it correctly.[3]

I have another experiment for you to try. Stand up and walk to the wall near a doorway. Take a front stance, so that your weight is 50-50. Put your fist out so that it is touching a wall, and lock your elbow. I know this is not how you punch, but we need to control the variables so that you can see what I am talking about. Keeping your forearm parallel to the floor, elbow up so it is pointing to another wall, palm facing the floor, and horizontal to the floor. Watch your shoulder. Tighten your arm and shoulder muscles and transfer your weight to your front foot.

You should be able to move forward two or three inches before your shoulder locks down again and stops your forward motion. If you do not experience this shock absorber, one of three things is happening: (1) you are not transferring your weight, but you are just trying to use muscle; (2) you are a power lifter capable of lifting your own body weight; or (3) you are doing it correctly and dropping your shoulder to establish structure.

---

3. I once joked with a muay Thai fighter, who had over 200 professional fights, that the only way I would step into the ring with him was wearing full-plate armor, with pillows duct-taped on top of that. His laughing response was, "It will still hurt." It was poetry in motion to watch this man's mastery of the Big 3. When he hit the bags, the rafters shook. You don't stand there and take a hit from this kind of person.

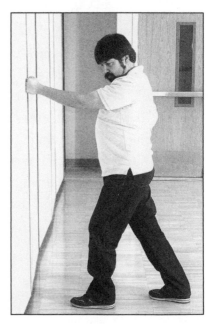

Front stance, straight punch looking at shoulder.

If the last is the case, good for you. Dipping your shoulder is a component of creating structure that most people unconsciously neglect. Without lowering it, your shoulder will collapse in, until it finds another structural position.

Another way to establish structure is to turn your elbow toward the floor. In both cases you should not be able to transfer your weight forward without intentionally collapsing your arm.

I want you to turn your elbow horizontal again, bending your arm. Don't drop your shoulder, but lock down your muscles. Now transfer your weight. You're going to feel all kinds of force. This is what most people feel when they think they are hitting hard. Their lack of structure makes the force coming back at them feel as if they are really delivering power. Now compare that to how it feels when you have structure and attempt to transfer your weight. Yes, you can feel it, but it is far less work, even though you are delivering more force into the wall.

Not only does this exercise demonstrate everything that I mean by structure and shock absorbers, but it also shows you how a matter of inches can rob you of your structure. Realize that different types of punches have different "correct" structures. Quite often this depends on the range where the punch is designed to deliver force. In fact, many of the faster sport punches don't really have any structure until the very end of the movement and at a great distance. Other types of punches lose structure if you attempt to strike outside their shorter range.

If you are in incorrect range and try to extend or contract your blow, *you will have to destroy your structure*.

Position yourself again in that front stance in front of the wall with your weight distributed 50-50. Keeping your shoulder dropped with your punch, position yourself so that when you put your fist out, it is about an inch away from the wall. Lift your shoulder. Your fist will now reach the wall—at the cost of your structure.

It is here that you have a choice. You can either destroy your structure by lifting your shoulder, or, keeping it down, transfer your weight forward. People do the former all the time. Then they bitch that the move didn't work, and so they need to find something else that does.

I said it before and I will say it again: *Power, when correctly applied, will have an effect. A move that lacks power and is misapplied won't.* If you are sacrificing your structure to compensate for being in the wrong position, it doesn't matter what style, system, or techniques you use.

Although the nature of structure remains consistent, the means of accomplishing it vary according to style, system, or even what you are attempting to accomplish. In other words, karate achieves structure differently than wing chun; silat does it differently than defensive tactics; judo or grappling do it using different means altogether. But they all use it. While I can give you the overall standards that must be met, the exact details and how you achieve them depend on your training.

I will tell you right up front that the information is already there, inside the system you know or are learning. Question Number One is: Has it been brought out and thoroughly examined, was it glossed over or poorly explained, or was it assumed that you would *learn as you go?* Rushing past the basics and moving on to the exciting flash moves is all too common in both martial arts and defensive tactics training. The problem is that the fundamentals are sacrificed in doing so.

If you don't find corollaries or similar information in your training, what you have been taught is sport sparring. This is not designed for power transfer into your opponent, but rather for speed. In a sport context, speed is more important than power, but that is not something you want to use in an actual confrontation.

Question Number Two is: How much time have you spent focusing on perfecting the component parts, or have you just assumed that a technique is a homogenized whole? Did you assume that by simply doing the action, *everything would fall in line*? Even the simplest tasks have component parts. In order to be good at the task, you must dwell on each of those components individually.

The preceding paragraphs were not an attempt to blame anyone. They were very much an attempt to point out how, if you don't pay attention to the components, it will be nearly impossible for you to learn them—much less remember to apply them in a violent encounter. If your instructor didn't emphasize these components, there is no way that you can realize how important they are to effective offense. You have to make understanding them your priority.

I'd like you to go back and do the range-finding exercise on the bag again. In a fighting stance start working your way in, from too far out to too close, and try to hit the vertical axis. Do not transfer your weight; instead, intentionally sacrifice your structure in order to reach the target. You will feel the difference. A blow delivered from the correct range and with your body in the correct pose *will have structure*. A blow that doesn't meet these building codes will collapse.

Now, with this in mind, try stepping into range, transferring your weight and hitting with structure. When you do this, you will be hitting correctly and transferring power into the bag. When you are working on the bag in the future, make these components your focus. In time, controlling these factors will become almost instinctive. When that happens, all your blows will deliver maximum power.

What I have just talked about is impacts, punching, and kicking. However, I also stated that structure is a much bigger topic. I'd like to briefly address some of the other manifestations.

A good way to show you how unaware we are of the significance of structure—and how much we rely on it unconsciously—can be found in a simple, one-minute exercise. Stand for thirty seconds; just find a comfortable position and count to thirty. You should be able to do this without problem or strain.

Next, squat down as though you were sitting in a chair that is not there. Try to maintain that position for thirty seconds. Even if you can, there will be significant muscle strain and tension.

The same amount of weight is being controlled in both instances—unless you somehow managed to magically gain fifty pounds. In the first, your skeleton and its structure are taking most of the weight. What little muscle is being used is applied to keep your joints from folding. You have literally braced yourself against gravity, using your skeleton.

In the second instance, your muscles alone are holding your weight in place. Yes, they are working around the skeleton, but now they, not your skeleton, are doing all the work. In simple terms, your support structure is gone and you must do all the work yourself. This is why it tires and strains you so quickly.

Understanding the importance of structure is not only critical for force delivery, but also is a key element of relaxing in soft styles. The reason proper body posture is important is that it creates structure that allows you to relax your muscles as much as possible. Relaxed muscles are fast muscles; tight, clenched muscles are not able to move quickly at all. If you are not in the correct pose, you cannot relax. You can stay there, but you will have to tighten your muscles to do so.

Recognizing proper body posture is essential for learning about structure. The litmus test is: Are you relaxed?

I have a demonstration that I use to teach this concept. I have students stand in a relaxed, normal stance. I ask them if they are relaxed. Usually, they will answer yes. The truth is, if they were totally relaxed they would be lying on the floor because their joints would have folded. They are, however, as relaxed as they can be in a standing position.

Now—and this qualifier is important—without sticking their butts out to counterbalance, I have them lean forward and stay there. I ask if they are relaxed now. They won't be.

This simple exercise teaches that we can stay in nonstructurally supported poses, but we won't be relaxed. We must tighten our muscles in order to hold those postures. In doing so we slow down any attempted movement.

Here is where things really get stupid. In order to compensate for a lack of range and structure, people commonly try to "patch" with muscle. Instead of using correct physics, they try to make the move work by using brute strength.

It's time for another exercise. Stand up. Lock down every muscle you have, to the point that even your teeth are clenched. Look like the Incredible Hulk, with every muscle bulging and flexed.

Now walk forward.

You can't do it. You will have to relax some muscles in order to move. Even then, your movements will be about as quick as molasses in January. I cannot begin to tell you how important this silly exercise is. This is exactly how many people think they are going to generate power. They tense up and try to throw everything they have at their opponent.

To watch them try to do this as fast as they can is where it really gets absurd. They are trying to patch their lack of the Big 3 (range, structure, and body movement) with so many things that their coherent body movement just disintegrates. When you mix being too tight with trying to move fast with extra movement to get more power, being horribly out of range, and making power come from your hips, you get the Funky Chicken dance of an untrained fighter.

Most people who lose power try to generate more. That's like trying to fix a decaying radio signal by turning up the volume: "The transmission isn't getting through; turn it up!"

Unfortunately, the idea of patching your technique with muscle is such a common failing that some schools insist that you must be in prime physical condition in order to be effective at offense. They actually emphasize this conditioning over skill. They teach students to rely on physical conditioning to give them the ability to take a greater amount of punishment in order to win.

Unfortunately, because they assume that they can *take it*, such players seldom pay attention to the concept of fence. Why bother to learn to move when you can tough it out? Because of this blindness, they are the first to go down when weapons are involved.

I should also point out it is true that mass and muscle will commonly compensate for poor technique—until you go up against someone who is as strong and in as good a shape as you are; or, worse, bigger and stronger. Then this approach doesn't work anymore. Where it totally falls down is when you encounter someone with greater skill.

I would like you to think about stories you might have heard (or may even have experienced) about little old masters who dribble larger, stronger, and younger students. It seems as though these little old men and women don't even move at all, and the burly student goes flying. A major reason these clichés exist is because these things do happen. They happen because these little old masters know about the Big 3 and fence.

To begin with, you will notice that these individuals always move into range. This is one of the most critical components of maintaining correct structure: *Put yourself in the right place!* The most common destroyer of structure is being in the wrong range and trying to make the move work anyway. By trying to reach out and compensate for those extra inches, you take yourself out of a structural pose. You've just put in shock absorbers.

If you have quality training—that is, if you were taught by someone who knew how to transfer power—you learned how to do a move in a structural manner. The correct way to do a move will, most often, give you structural integrity. If you operate within that move's range, you will have structure. It is when you attempt to do it outside of its range that you destroy structure.

The exceptions to this are sports moves. By sports moves I mean point-sparring techniques that rely on speed and merely attempt to make contact with an opponent in order to score a point, not to deliver power. The defining characteristics of point-sparring moves are the positioning of the limbs, the lack of body movement, their generation through muscle only, their tendency to leave you wide open, the lack of balance, and their shaky grasp of range.

An example of this kind of move is what was called the California backfist, in which the person jumps forward and snaps a quick, fast, light backfist to the top of his sparring partner's headgear. It is a point-generating move that is incredibly fast (which is why it is used to spook your opponent to keep him from closing on you). It is not, however, a blow that has range, structure, or coordinated body movement behind it, although with some practice it could be.

My point is that the old masters move into range and their structure then allows that body movement to be turned into force that is delivered into their opponent. It also allows them to handle incoming force from their opponent without being knocked over, which is another wonderful benefit of structure.

~ 7 ~

Faith and Tactical Application

Your thinking is done
during your training.

—Old Special Forces maxim

By simply focusing on understanding the Big 3 during your training, you will have resolved a great many of the problems that tend to manifest themselves in a violent encounter. When you combine them with fence, many more problems fade away.

However, one of the biggest problems is not external, it is internal. By mastering the Big 3 and fence you will have begun to develop what I call *faith*. That very simple word has a profound effect on how you mount an offense.

Lt. Col. David Grossman, in his book *On Killing*, proposed a fantastic model of human reaction to danger—a very specific type of danger, from another human. He replaces the old fight/flight model with four possible reactions: fight, flight, posture (threat display), and submit.

In a private conversation, he mentioned that if he were to redo it, he would replace "submit" with "freeze."

I disagree, and one of these days we're going to have to have a sit down over a cup of coffee and argue this point. My reason for saying this is that I don't think freeze is a replacement, but an addition. Instead of having a four-part model, you have five; not as elegant, but, I feel, more accurate.

I consider there to be distinct differences between submission (surrendering) and "freezing." Both are very specific actions. I suspect that they arise from related, but different, sources.

I maintain that there is no male on this planet who has not faced *The Choice*. It's very simple. It's the realization that you have an immediate decision to make: swallow pride or swallow blood.

It is knowing beyond a shadow of a doubt that the other side outguns you. It is knowing that you aren't going to win if you try to fight, whether the situation involves keeping your mouth shut and letting a group of bullies cut in front of you in the school lunch line, surrendering to the enemy and becoming a prisoner of war, or biting your tongue to keep from getting fired when your boss is yelling at you. It's about shutting up and putting up with what is happening.

Quite honestly, some people will always put pride first. They will neither surrender nor back down. They have to say something, no matter what the cost. Their pride demands that they get in that last dig. Once, during a phone interview with a radio talk show host, I was asked if there were something she could say to let a criminal who was robbing her know how upset she was with him. I told her no, such an action would commonly provoke him to pull the trigger. She objected to this idea and proceeded to argue for her emotional right to tell the guy off. A former gang member called up and told her I was right: had she done that to him, he would have shot her. She still insisted on her need to express her outrage, even though her pride and anger would have gotten her killed.

Like running a stop sign at 80 miles an hour, some people go speeding by the moment of choice with nary a glance. Quite often they pay the consequences of their insistence. Depending on the circumstances, they either bleed, die, get fired, or are socially ostracized for this behavior.

Most people, however, choose submission.

My point is that it is a conscious choice, when faced with overwhelming force, to not resist. There are distinct behavioral patterns associated with it. In my experience, submission comes in two main flavors. The first is knowing you are not going to win, and if you try to resist there is a good chance you will be seriously hurt, or killed. Therefore, you agree to cooperate, in hopes of surviving.

The second is that you have something more important than your pride to consider, and you choose not to resist. This is why, when you have a family to support, you don't tell an obnoxious boss to take this job and shove it. You instead bow your head and submit.

The act of submission often requires you to position your body in such a way that you do not send aggressive posturing signals. A surrendering soldier holds his hands up and away from his body. A person who is not arguing or contesting holds his arms down at his sides and lowers his head and, possibly, his eyes. These are submissive postures designed to prevent an attack by not provoking it through actions that could be interpreted as defiance.[1]

That's submission. Now what about freezing?

It has been both my observation and experience that freezing comes in two flavors as well. The first is tactical; that is to say, the complete and utter cessation of movement is a conscious choice for a tactical objective. This can mean the kind of freezing you do when you unexpectedly encounter a large predator. You don't move, in hopes of its not seeing you. Another kind of tactical freezing occurs when you are walking through a rice paddy on patrol and step on something that goes *click*. In that instance you freeze to prevent any damage.

In both cases the freeze is a conscious reaction to an incoming stimulus. Does it provide prep time to prepare for a fight or come up with a workable plan? Yes. Does it offer time to wildly hope that you don't have to enact that plan? You betcha. Nobody is saying that it isn't scary, but both are cases of freezing with a purpose.

The second type of freezing is what I call *lack freezing*. By this I mean that the *person freezes because he or she doesn't have a reliable solution to the problem at hand.*

This is often where one type of freezing segues into another, i.e., what was initially a tactical freeze becomes an inability to act.

---

1. I should point out that in typical alpha-beta behavior (social hierarchy and group dynamics) this is a signal for the aggression to end or, at least, begin to slacken. Dominance has been established and the offending behavior rectified. However, if the individual does not understand the nature of leadership (alpha behavior), he will instead decide to increase the level of attack when submission is shown—often as punishment for the offense. This shows a serious flaw in the character of the aggressor or that the surrender signal was sent too late. The social contract stipulates that when a person submits, the dominator stops attacking. Violation of these rules by both sides is the source of all kinds of violence.

Now this lack could reflect a total absence of any kind of plan. In that case the brain just shuts down because what a person is facing is so big and beyond his or her scope that the person just stands there dumfounded. Having interviewed a number of mugging victims, I find that this is an extremely common response to being robbed. There the person was, one second heading for her car and thinking about what to cook for dinner, and the next, looking down the barrel of a gun. That sudden change was so great and so shocking that the person had no frame of reference for it.

In such a situation people's brains shut down. They don't know what to do and often are unable to even make a sound. They are so outside their normal circumstances that they have no emergency plans the amygdala can implement. The amygdala is part of what Killology Research Group Grossman so appropriately calls the "puppy brain." The puppy brain is the part that we use in a crisis. It is not as smart as our "higher brain." In fact, it tends to operate on autopilot, based on what it knows. But if it has no preexisting response, it shorts out, and the person ends up standing there motionless. How does this apply to freezing? If the amygdala doesn't accept the training, you freeze.

In the old neurological model, stimuli came in and were processed through the higher brain. Then, orders were sent to the amygdala—which, incidentally, controls your adrenalin. Research by Joseph LeDoux discovered a "back alley" that leads straight to the amygdala, which means that in a crisis, stimuli feed directly into it.

It appears that the amygdala not only has generalized definitions of *known* dangers, but also programmed responses. Essentially, if you recognize A, then you react 1, 2, 3. If you recognize B, you react 4, 5, 6. If the message coming in through the back alley is a known danger, your body will automatically react according to these plans. This is often the basis of what Dr. Daniel Goleman calls "emotional hijacking" in his book *Emotional Intelligence*. When the amygdala perceives a danger, it initiates a programmed emotional reaction—regardless of whether it is appropriate.

Now think about this from a survival standpoint: If your instincts tell you to run up a tree when you see a tiger, you have both a designation of danger and an automatic response. If you see anything that even looks like a tiger, your body kicks into gear and you are up a tree. Using your puppy brain, this happens long before your conscious mind can think about it and decide, "Well, it looks like a tiger. Perhaps we should saunter over and contemplate climbing the tree." This is not how you stay alive in tiger country. You need an automatic re-action pattern to known dangers. At the first hint of a tiger's presence, you are heading at full tilt toward that tree. Conscious thought comes back as you are sitting in the branch, wondering what tipped you off that Sher Khan (from Kipling) was in the 'hood.

The nice thing about the amygdala is that it is program-mable to the environment. An Eskimo doesn't need to worry about tigers, but he does have to worry about polar bears. We learn to recognize dangers that are common to our environment and ingrain effective solutions. It is those solutions we will automatically enact when we encounter the situation.

Problems occur, however, when there is a situation outside these known parameters, and the person tries to react according to the old rules. It is also why, in a crisis, people often continue to repeat an ineffective response, such as continuing to push brakes when sliding on ice, or beat a locked door's push bar during a fire. Paramedics will tell you about the weird things people do in crises. From a calm outside perspective these actions may seem stupid, but these behaviors usually involve groping to find an appropriate response.

That is why, when faced with something extreme and so outside their normal operating parameters, that people tend to freeze. Their emergency response team doesn't have a clue as to how to deal with this kind of problem. The only thing they have going at that moment is fear, fear that has grown into panic.

That is one kind of freezing: you just don't know what to do. Quite simply, this kind can be overcome by training and drilling. A teacher ingrains a set and proven response, then has the students practice it. This way, if something happens they at least have some idea of what to do.

This, I should point out, is the difference between fear and panic. This is only my definition and not necessarily the ultimate truth, but I make an important distinction between fear and panic. With fear, you know what to do; the question is, can you do it fast enough?

With panic, you don't know what to do, so it destroys any chance of appropriate action. Without the availability of a proven effective response, fear takes over and turns into panic.

Fear is your friend, panic is your enemy. Fear will help you get to your goal faster. Panic will either shut you down or send you down an inappropriate course of action for the situation (like yelling obscenities at the mugger for pointing a gun at you).

Unfortunately, fear has a bad rap. It has become confused with panic in many self-defense programs. The resulting goal, in some cases, is to train for *no fear*. This is a mistake. In fact, it is hogwash.

Fear is a motivational message, and it should be used to enhance your actions in order to achieve a goal. Even under frightening conditions, a person with enough experience and the proper training can act and can accomplish complex processes.

The example I use in seminars starts with asking how many parents are in the room. Then I paint a scenario: Your child is hurt and unconscious; what do you do? Immediately, there is an avalanche of answers. What is interesting to note is that not only are solutions to the crisis delineated with machine-gun rapidity, but they often involve complex tasks—tasks that you can bet your bottom dollar would be executed (e.g., driving to the emergency room).

I want you to realize that driving is a skill that is practiced daily. As such, there is a good chance that people can still perform it under fear or stress conditions; maybe not as well as they normally would, but they can get the job done. In contrast, tasks that are not routinely practiced tend to go awry especially in the presence of fear or stress.

The critical component, however, is a clearly defined goal the practiced task achieves. The goal is not the complex act itself (e.g., driving is not the goal but getting the child to the emergency room is). If you do not have a clearly defined goal beyond the task itself, you will fail to perform. It doesn't matter if you are going 120 mph if you don't know where you are going.

I mention that because such goals as defending myself or winning a fight are in fact *fuzzy goals*. They are not clearly defined, tactical goals. It may not seem so while sitting in the comfort of your chair or even standing in the training ring, but reality is revealed in actual confrontation.

This brings us back to the puppy brain and how well it is trained. It only understands clearly defined goals. Get up the tree, get to a hospital. These are goals it understands and uses its training to achieve. "Defending myself" is too vague an idea to allow the puppy brain to know which plan to put into effect.

This creates a break of effective action, resulting in either wild flailing or, just as often, freezing.

Is the freeze total? Not always. In fact, I have seen many occasions when someone who is being assaulted simply curls up. It is the best idea that they can come up with, and they literally freeze into trying to run that program. The same can be said of someone who continually tries to make an ineffective technique work. Instead of freezing, the person is looping like a computer caught in a bad program.

The second cause of freezing stems from what I call *a lack of faith*. Put simply, *If you have been trained but don't trust your training, you won't do it.*

If you don't believe—down to your toes—that your training will work to keep you safe, there is a good chance you will freeze. If you don't freeze, there is an even better chance that you will only attempt a half-hearted technique. What should be a bone-shattering technique devolves into a flailing, childish slap.

I have seen countless manifestations of failure to perform, everything from a total meltdown into a human statue; to gibbering, screaming panic; to hiding behind something and cowering; to posturing and threat displays when someone should be engaging in combat actions; to hesitation before joining combat; to half-hearted offenses while engaged in a conflict; to an individual's hanging back while his teammates charge in. (In the last case, the person who hung back is usually the first one to tell the brass how he brilliantly handled the whole situation.)

A lack of faith comes in many forms. No matter how it manifests, it stems from the person's not trusting his or her training to get the job done.

I use the term *faith* for some very specific reasons. I'm not talking about blind faith here. Nor am I talking about fanaticism.

There is an old saying, "You're not fanatical about something that you are sure about." Unfortunately, that saying applies in spades to a great many people in the reality-based self-defense world and those who claim to study combat arts. They are fanatical about how deadly their fighting styles are. When you hear them start talking, just remember that old saying about fanaticism. If they were so sure, they'd be doing more and talking less.

My point is, you never meet a fanatic about the fact that the sun will rise tomorrow or that gravity works. That is the kind of faith I am talking about. You know it will happen. You need to know that if you meet certain building codes, you will have the best chance of not getting hurt.

The reason I use the word *faith* is that, at first, you have to take this information on faith. When I tell you that range, body movement, and structure are critical to power transfer, I am asking you to take *on faith* that these issues are worth your time to investigate. But that is where faith ends and hard science begins.

From there on, it is a matter of demonstrable, provable study and experimentation. You not only have to learn it, but you have to know it works and why. By this I don't mean that your forebrain thinks that by being ranked in a fighting style means you know how to fight. I mean that your puppy brain knows it works. You have to have a calm assurance—based on experience—that if you meet these building codes it will work.

I am talking about knowing, if you meet the standards of a move, what will happen and having the same amount of doubt about those results that you have about the sun coming up. For example, I know beyond a shadow of a doubt that if I break someone's structure or balance and prevent him from reestablishing a base, he will fall. I know this because I know gravity works. If I meet these conditions, he is going to fall down. It is guaranteed because of the laws of physics.

I may not trust a martial arts style, but I have faith in the laws of physics. So that is what I am going to put my money on.

I tell you this because thinking this way gives you priorities. It gives you immediate goals that your puppy brain can grasp and, with training, drilling, and experience, immediately achieve. It knows it works, it knows safety is there when you do it, and in a crisis it is going to make sure it happens.

It is the person who goes into a conflict with both short- and long-term goals—and whose short-term goals are proven, progressive steps in achieving that long-term goal—who will win.

That is the person whose conscious and emotional mind, and puppy brain will be working together to achieve a goal that can be achieved, and once achieved will have positive results.

What I really want you to consider is the correlation between these psychological aspects and what I discussed earlier about the component parts of effective power delivery. You cannot achieve a greater goal without having first studied and practiced the steps to get there.

It is not the technique that generates power. Making sure you have all the component parts in the move allows you to generate and deliver power through that technique. In the same way you must understand your own psychology in order to mount an effective offense. If a part of you distrusts what you "think you know," under stress you will freeze or hesitate. It is that lack of faith that hinders you.

You have to look at the psychology of what you are doing and how you are training. You are training your conscious brain and you are trying to train your puppy brain. As a dog has different priorities, thought processes, and instincts from yours, your puppy brain thinks differently from your conscious mind. That can make most training a hard sell, because it sees things differently.

I often say that the puppy brain is from Missouri. It lives in the Show-Me State, which is not a place, but a state of mind. Before it believes something it has to be shown that it works. I'm not referring to a slick sales pitch, but to something reliably and consistently proven (e.g., gravity has got a great track record). It has to have faith that it works and it has to know it can do it. You may accept that in the sparring ring a move works 60 percent of the time. But that dog won't hunt. Your amygdala isn't going to forget that other 40 percent—especially before it commits itself to using that move in a situation where you could be killed. And if you try to force it, it will fight you all the way.

This brief discourse on psychology should have a major influence on how you look at your training. You need to focus on finding the critical components that make your tactics work. When you recognize and focus on ingraining them into your reactions, you will begin to prove to your puppy brain that they work. When that happens, you are far more likely to organize your priorities and make sure that you accomplish them—even under stress.

Issues such as stress, the physical effects of adrenalin, tunnel vision, time distortion, and auditory exclusion will have a serious impact on your performance. Anything that is not ingrained in your midbrain and skills will deteriorate under these conditions. If those skills are based on solid building codes, you should be able to achieve your goals anyway.

This is the cornerstone of faith. By training to ingrain those elements that allow for effective power delivery you are far more likely to make sure they are included in both your offensive and defensive movement. This in kata, sparring training, and, most importantly, live-fire situations. Your puppy brain will do what it knows works—and it will do so with total commitment.

Let us for a moment look at the importance of this in light of adrenal stress.[2] Yes there will be a decay of motor skills in an actual conflict. But let's say you have the Big 3 ingrained in how you move. Meet this criteria and a move has a 100 percent success rate. If you don't have them ingrained, it—at best—has a 50/50 chance (this even in the safety of a sparring ring). Let's assign a random negative 30 percent value to adrenal stress. That means a value of 30 percent is automatically subtracted because of the stress and strain of it being a "real" fight. Thirty percent from 100 gives you a possible success rate of 70 percent. While a move without the Big 3, when hit with this 30 percent penalty has only a 20 percent chance of success. What would you rather put your faith in to save your life: 70 percent or 20 percent chance of success? Those odds are what your puppy brain is looking at, even if you aren't.

You must calculate this as you train, focus, and drill. By planning for this deterioration, you will learn to focus on issues that do not fall apart, aspects that work no matter how stressed you are.

Unfortunately, current training, especially in martial arts and defensive tactics, does not address what it takes to train the amygdala. It might train your conscious mind, but until you train your hind brain using proven effective information and tactics, and then practice applying those under stressful conditions, you will not be able to perform.

If there is any chance of finding yourself in a live-fire situation, you must look into this very important subject. I cannot stress enough the importance of making sure you have trained in such a manner as to create faith in what you know and can do. There is entirely too much training out there that does not

---

2. See Peyton Quinn's *Real Fighting.*

adequately address this subject. Instructors just assume that by knowing the physical techniques, you will be able to apply them in combat.

What I can point out is that the U.S. military has studied this problem for 200 years and spent billions of dollars trying to perfect ways to train effective fighting men. If they think it is worth that much time, money, and study to create training systems that will produce someone who can function effectively in combat, then you might want to look into it—instead of just assuming that by knowing a fighting style you will be able to function in a violent confrontation.

As the chapter quote says, your thinking is done in training. That also means to make sure that your training focuses on the things that will keep you alive in an actual confrontation (unlimited offense), not just allow you to win in the safety of a sparring match (limited offense).

~ 8 ~

Blocking and Deflecting

No matter how enmeshed a commander becomes in the elaboration of his own thoughts, it is sometimes necessary to take the enemy into account.

—Winston Churchill

I have a warning for people who get too wrapped up in what they are planning to do to an opponent. I tell them, "It's a different game when the other side shoots back." When they hear this, people with lots of training but little experience look at me like I am a total idiot. Obviously I don't realize what dangerous fighters they are because they know who-flung-poo-fu—a fighting system of such deadly superiority that their opponent will never have a chance to counterattack. Ah, the confidence of the inexperienced.

Important safety tip here: If you are in a situation where you are justified in using physical force (i.e., you need effective offense), you also are in a situation where the other guy is a danger—often because he is attacking you. The need for effective offense is based on the simple fact that you have to stop him from hurting you (or someone else).

Many years of dealing with violence has taught me that incoming fire has a tendency to mess up your offensive plans. There are two main reasons. First, it can make you nervous. When you realize with bowel-clenching certainty that someone is seriously trying to hurt you—and there is nothing between that attack and you except air—you might get a little flustered.

Second, if you have not focused on making sure that your moves meet code, there is a good chance that your offense is going to get tangled up in his. The next thing you know, you are left standing in close proximity to someone who wants to hurt you, with no reliable plan of action. This tends to complicate things, trust me on this.

This, of course, assumes that his offense doesn't just render you unconscious or knock your teeth out. Unconsciousness or severe pain tends to take your mind off launching an effective offense. Having to wing it because your offense got tangled up is hard enough, but coming up with a new and effective offense when you are in a world of hurt is nearly impossible.

When it comes to defense, many people are fishing for minnows while standing on the back of a whale. Because they cannot see the bigger issue, they make all kinds of erroneous assumptions about the nature of defense. These are the minnows they are fishing for while ignoring the whale. And that whale of an answer is going to reach up and smack them silly. I'm not speaking metaphorically here, either. Before you even think of launching an effective offense, you have to make sure that your opponent's offense won't foil your attempts.

This brings us to things like blocking, deflecting, parrying, and countering as an integral part of developing fence. They are instrumental in clearing your path so you can safely move to where you need to be.

I have heard a lot of instructors talk about targeting. Usually, they are talking about where to punch in order to get the most bang for your buck. But I want to take a look at that idea from the other side; not just from the perspective of where your attacks are going, but of where his are headed. Unless you are interested in having your nose driven through the back of your skull, you might want to ask yourself a very important question: In a larger sense, *where is his attack targeted?*

I'm talking not just about his trying to bust your face with a right hook, but about a more general and—to you—useful angle. It's very important to ask this question. It has an answer that will reorganize your priorities about defense.

So what is this bigger idea I keep hinting about? You already know that any offense has a particular range in which it delivers maximum power. That brings another dimension to targeting. It is no longer a line, but a location. It doesn't matter exactly what the offense is; your attacker is hoping that the move will deliver its payload at a particular spot. That is his primary target.

That spot just so happens to be where you are standing.

Well, duh! However, there is an extremely valid reason for stepping back and looking at this seemingly absurd idea. That statement sounds silly only until you realize that failing to move from that spot is one of the biggest reasons you will get your butt kicked.

When you see an attack coming, don't brace to take the impact, as so many people do—*Move!* If you don't move from that spot, there is a very good chance that his attack is going to land. And it will land with as much force as he can muster. This is likely to happen even if you try to block. If your block is in the wrong place or doesn't get there in time, the attack will still get through.

Unfortunately, this bigger question of *where the blow is heading* is often lost in the details of fussing over what kind of block to use against what kind of attack. People are so busy trying to figure out what defense to use that they don't realize they are standing in the same spot while contemplating the problem.

That's an example of the minnow/whale analogy I made earlier.

It is glaringly obvious who has and who hasn't realized the three-dimensional nature of targeting. Your vertical axis is an intersecting line that forms a point on the line of his attack. How high or low they meet forms the third line. Three lines are what you need to find coordinates in 3-D space. His attack provides two of those lines, your VA is the third. That is why I say a target is a location, a place you need to move from. People who haven't realized this stand there and get pummeled during fights, and even in sparring matches. What is most shocking is how surprised they are they are getting hit—even though they are blocking. I am not joking about how obvious it will become. In time you will want to literally scream, "MOVE, STUPID!" at someone who digs in when attacked.

You need to move your body not only to generate force for your offense, but also to reduce his effectiveness and protect yourself against his offense. The trick isn't to do only this, but to deploy defensive hand work at the beginning of your fence move. It is initially defensive, but it turns offensive near the end. Defensive hand work clears the path for you to move into range—while at the same time putting yourself into a position where he cannot launch another attack at you.

Your defensive hand work doesn't just keep you from getting hit, but keeps going ahead to make sure he doesn't move where you need to be. It checks him from moving to a tactically advantageous position, while allowing you to do just that. If not moving is the primary source of getting hit the first time, failing to check him from moving back into attack position is the main reason people get hit by the second attack.

It is possible to do all of these with what is functionally one move. When you get to this point, the first part of your move is defensive, the middle involves moving into position, and the last part constitutes a devastating offensive move. You've seen this idea before; it's called fence. But you are not going to develop this skill without a lot of skull sweat and practice.

For now let's look at the benefits of moving from where you are standing when he attacks. Entirely too many people freeze like a deer in the headlights, allowing that attack to be delivered full force. Or, just as bad, they stay in the exact location and attempt to block. Both responses are sure ways not only of getting hit, but of getting hit as hard as possible.

I want you to think about these reactions in two different ways. First, think of them in the context of not having faith in what you are doing. How much faith are you going to have in a process that is only marginally successful? Yet every time you don't move (i.e., every time you get hit), it is going to erode your confidence in your block. This also will increase your chances of freezing, hesitating, tightening up, overreacting, or destroying your structure by moving too fast or with too much muscle. The less faith you have in your ability, the more mistakes you are going to make. Where I'm from, we call that a self-fulfilling prophecy.

The second way I want you to look at it is that if you don't move, you are literally assisting him to develop range, body movement, and structure. Yep, by staying there, you have just improved his chances of developing enough power to hurt you. That is what we are going to talk about right now.

Just by moving from where his attack is targeted, you will exploit his weaknesses in the Big 3. Put simply, not only do you lessen the chances of being struck, but even if you are hit, you will have seriously decreased the power of his attack. As you have seen, correct range is critical for effective power delivery. You are robbing him of power by changing ranges against that particular attack. And if he doesn't understand range, there is an even better chance that he doesn't understand structure. So, if he hits you while you are moving, his structure collapses. Even if your block misses, just by stepping into the incorrect range for his attack you are going to play hob with his attempts to hurt you.

I used to demonstrate this by having people punch me in the chest. I would stand there, let them get into correct range, and hit me. Then I would tell them to deliver the same blow again, but to hit me as hard as they could. I am talking about trying to cave in my chest. As they started the blow, without blocking I would step into them. I often wouldn't even have to bump chests. My incoming force meeting their punch before it could reach optimum range would knock them backward. In any case, their structure collapsed against my incoming mass, rendering their blow ineffective just by changing range on them.

This is exactly why, in a limited-offense situation (i.e., where there are no complicating factors), a grappler can—and most often will—take down an impact fighter. The person charging has greater momentum. Against a blow, especially one where the puncher's structure is weak, the greater mass plows through. This is especially true because of the retraction of an impact. The person charging in will follow the retreating fist back to the puncher's body.[1]

---

1. This is why drives work better to keep rushers at a distance. You not only don't let them follow your retreating hand back in, but you put structure between you and them.

Am I advocating charging straight in? No. That is a tactic that works well in certain limited-offense circumstances. It is not safe to try against an unlimited offense. It is definitely not a survival strategy when facing a total offense. It has its time and place, but nowhere near as often as people try to make it work. What is important, however, is that you *practice destroying an attacker's effectiveness through movement.* There are many ways to do this other than straight in.

An exercise will help you learn about this, while also ingraining movement as a reaction to an incoming attack. To perform this exercise, you need a chest protector (hogue), a partner, and hand wraps. Your partner wears the wraps and you wear the hogue. Pick a particular punch. At first have your partner throw this punch into your chest from correct range. Don't have him step; just have him stand in range when he fires. It should rattle you to your socks. Then, as he throws the blow, without blocking try moving into different positions. Compare the degree of force that you receive while moving against the blow you took while stationary.[2] Trade equipment and have him move. As he does, pay close attention to how much power you lose when he moves to different positions and ranges.

The next level of this exercise requires that your partner not screw around and try to count coup on you. It is important for training purposes for him to launch only one punch per engagement. He steps into range, fires, and steps back. You will not block. In fact, you should either cross your hands in front or behind or you tuck them against your chest, like a boxer guarding too closely. Your partner's target is again your hogue-covered chest. Pick three different ranges for punches: far, middle, close.

---

2. It is important that your partner remain on his original target and not correct to strike you in your new position.

It doesn't matter which hand delivers the blow. What does matter is *that only one blow is thrown per engagement.* It also matters that your partner understands the importance of range and thus knows how to throw the correct punch for the distance.

Have your partner stand just outside punching range. At his discretion, he steps into a particular range and fires off the appropriate punch. His job is to land it. Yours is to foil that attempt by moving—not by blocking.

There are many benefits to this exercise. Not the least is that it teaches you to start watching for his movement into range, not his fist flying at your face, as the indicator of an attack. More important, it ingrains the idea of moving when an attack is being launched as opposed to standing there and expecting to block it.

It is quite natural for horseplay to develop in this exercise. It is frustrating for your partner to be limited in his offense when you are so obviously open and all he has to do is add one more punch. Instead of trying to tell him not to do so, make that the final stage of this exercise. Only do this after you have learned how to move easily and are consistently bleeding the power from his attacks. Limit it to two attacks. You must shed not only one punch, but two, through movement.

I cannot stress enough the importance of waiting until you can consistently do this against one hit before moving to two blows. Don't rush it. It is the lack of body movement that will get you hit. It is the lack of focus on this aspect of training that causes it to be dropped from your defense in a live-fire situation. If you haven't spent time ingraining movement as part of your defensive attempts, you will freeze as if you were dipped in liquid nitrogen when attacked. This leaves you only with blocking as a means to protect yourself. You want to ingrain movement as your instinctive response to an attack.

Now that you understand the importance of movement in defense, we can begin to consider defensive hand work. In the model I use, there are four types of defensive moves: block, parry, deflect, and counter.

Before I go on, I want to point out why I make these differentiations. My attorney often says, "Everyone knows what something means until there is a problem." When it comes to misunderstanding defensive hand work, that statement applies in spades. Everyone knows what a block is . . . and everyone's definition is different. Sometimes what someone means by a block is what I would call a parry; other times it is a deflection. What is amazing is how often people don't realize that their definition is changing. They are using the same word to describe different things in the same conversation.

You know what? It's not their fault. In fact, definitions can be a little confusing even in the dictionary.

For purposes of communication, not as an attempt to set an industry standard, I am going to give you four definitions to clarify important—and different—concepts. What you call them or how you define them in your system is less important than your knowing the differences. These concepts, like other important ideas, work together. In fact, it will be a rare occurrence when you get one in a pure form. But, like other important concepts, they must be studied individually before you try to blend them.

At first glance, a block and a deflection look the same. That can be confusing. However, the difference between them is very much like that between driving and racing. Blocks and deflections use the same general action, but are applied differently. In fact, both use the same structure. Both are based in putting a structure between you and the incoming force. But even though they are structurally the same, their respective body movements create radically different results.

A *block* is based on either not moving or being pushed by the incoming force. A deflection occurs when you initiate the movement, moving either into or away from the blow. The defining difference is whether you initiate the body movement or not.

A *parry* is primarily based on speed and on deflecting the incoming force. Parries can be done, to borrow ideas from fencing, either as fast circular movements or what is called a *beat*. A beat occurs when you deal the incoming blow a fast, light strike to veer it off course. In either case, the parry hijacks the incoming force and deflects it. Parries do not necessarily need structure. They rely more on manipulating the incoming attack's inertia through speed. Obviously, this makes them faster than either blocks or deflections.

Counters are far more aggressive, in that they serve as stop hits, checks, derailment, counterpunches, or foils to your opponent's offense. They do not block or parry an incoming attack as much as they give it a flat tire before it can get started.[3] They do this at the source of the offense (i.e., they touch your opponent's body). Although you can use them as strikes, initially I want you to think of them first and foremost as throwing pebbles under the skateboard wheels of your attacker; or, for the rural types, think of yourself as the armadillo on his Texas highway of life.

I don't want you to focus too much on the hitting aspect of counters because you can easily fall into using them automatically as stop hits, checks or counterpunches. This is effective, but does not give you the same amount of control as deflection through positioning. Used in this manner, just by putting your hand in the right place you make him veer off course, as if you

---

3. As was pointed out to me, many people call these countering actions "check." A check is indeed very much a type of counter. Not all counters are checks, however, especially those that rely on deflection or creating a circular motion.

had shot out a tire on a speeding car he was driving. The direction in which he swerves is up to you.

I define these concepts in this manner because so many schools don't. In fact, I am not sure that many schools even understand that there are differences among them. Everything some schools know gets thrown into a giant grab bag that they call "blocking." Everyone uses this term, when in fact some people are blocking, others are parrying, and still others are countering. But everyone is absolutely sure that they know what the term *blocking* means.

As you will see, a block—the way most people do it—is the most ineffective means of defense. It is a move that, while it may save your butt, does not necessarily set you up for anything else, even if done correctly. It needs to be considered an emergency defensive move, not your first option.

A block commonly meets and defeats an incoming force. It can do this by either stopping the force or pushing it aside. No matter how it does either, however, a critical component must be present: structure.

Like blows, blocks must have structure. If they do not, they will collapse, especially under heavy incoming forces. Generally, structure is created with the upper arm, not the forearm. The upper arm is what must be in place to handle the incoming force. This simple statement can do wonders to increase your blocking effectiveness. The position of your upper arm and elbow is critical for the structural stability of your block and, by default, in determining how many times you get hit.

I would like you to do the following exercise with a partner. Have your partner stand in front of you and push against your forearms. Take a solid front stance with your back to a wall, and hold your arms in the following positions as though you were blocking.

 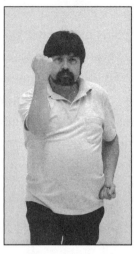 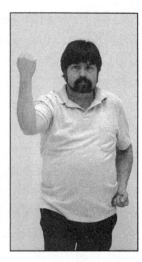

| *Outside block with elbow too far in.* | *Outside block with elbow in right spot.* | *Outside block with elbow too far out.* |

Putting his hand on your forearm, have him try to push toward the wall while you are in the above positions. He will be pushing into your blocks. One time, the force will be aimed at your right chest, a second time at your shoulder, and a third time would miss you entirely. After the first round, vary the part of your arm that he is pushing. One time have him put his hand on your wrist, another time on your elbow, then on your upper arm. You will discover that some positions collapse immediately, while others allow you to resist with ease.

Although these aren't the exact positions in which you will block, this exercise will show you the importance of structure in blocking (and by extension, in deflection). Take all the blocks that you know and experiment with them in this manner. Move your limbs to various positions close to where the blocks should be, and have someone push against them. If they collapse, it is a safe bet that you are in the wrong position and don't have structure. If you are in the position that you were taught and the block still collapses, the odds are that someone has tinkered with the system. Unfortunately, not all of the changes in modern martial arts are for the better. Errors have crept in; errors that rob you of your ability to handle incoming force. What you were taught might not give you structure either.

There are many reasons why blocks fail. The main one, however, is a combination of lack of structure and no movement. These two elements are so interconnected that they form a single yin-yang of disaster, each feeding into the other until they become one giant, whirling mess.

Take a look at a common reason why people fail to move. Many are stuck on the idea that a block stops an attack. In fact, they fixate on that idea. Unfortunately, there is a tendency in the West to overdo it. If a foot is good, then 10 feet are better. Thinking this way, they assume that *stop* or *push aside* means they must hit with their blocks.

This is the source of many problems. In trying to hit hard with their blocks, they often destroy their structure, speed past where they need to be, destroy their timing, and attempt to use muscle. In other words, they usually end up opening themselves wider to be hit.

Worst of all, in order to get all this power in their blocks, they unconsciously root themselves in the exact location where the attack is aimed. Put simply, they are standing there while their blocks are in the wrong place, at the wrong time—and they wonder why they get hit! Their usual response is to try to block harder and faster, which messes them up even more.

I am not saying that this cockamamie idea of trying to hit with your block is an attempt to compensate for weak structure, but if it looks like a duck, walks like a duck, and floats like a duck, it ain't a peacock. I won't say it is a duck yet, but I can say for sure that someone is trying to dress up an ineffective block in fancy tail feathers.

I want you to consider an alternative use for a block. That is, *to stall incoming force*.

Not to stop it, but to slow it down and bleed off energy until it has lost enough force that you can handle it by some other means. Remember I said that a block is more of an emergency stopgap? Use a block when you are unexpectedly attacked and don't have time to move beforehand.

The reason you don't need to stop a blow is because you are going to move. If you don't more, you will need perfect structure in order to absorb the incoming force. That structure must not only be in your arms, but in your entire body—especially your stance. Achieving perfect form with your entire body against a sudden and unexpected attack is difficult to the point of near impossibility.

What is not only possible, but probable (with a little bit of practice) is creating good enough structure with your arms to stall the attack long enough for you to move out of that location.

Try this exercise. Stand in an open area, with a partner in front of you. Have your partner push you. Don't worry about stance; just stand normally and let him push you. Don't fight it. Just let him move you around without losing your structure. Now do the same thing, but put your arm up into the "proper" position for a block and have him try to drive through it.

If your structure doesn't collapse, being pushed around is a common result. This is especially true when you meet superior mass with structure. Just let it push you instead of trying to fight it. The force has to go somewhere, and by walking backward you are bleeding it off. If you try to fight it, that force will go into you—with damaging or, at the very least, overwhelming effect.

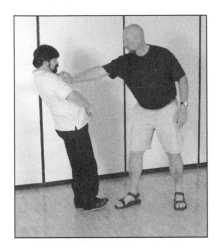 

Being tilted over—no. *Walking back with structure—yes.*

You will find that the only time your structure is broken or you are tipped over is when you try to resist.

The difference between being pushed with structure and being pushed over is that you move in balance with structure. This is not being pushed over. You are allowing his force to move you. He is literally pushing a car in neutral that rolls, but doesn't tip. You are sitting behind the wheel, letting him do all the work, and you decide when to put the car into gear again. In the meantime, "Thanks for the push, fella." I call this riding his force, "surfing" because like a surfer riding a wave, he may direct the general direction you are going, but you determine where in the wave you go.

Unfortunately, too many people try to block while staying in one place and trying to resist incoming pressure. When they do this, either their incorrect structure collapses, or they are bowled over, or both occur.

There are many ways the former can happen. The most obvious is when the blow continues to power past the block and hits its target. The block just doesn't have what it takes to affect the incoming blow. In other cases the block collapses against a rush, even though the blocker is in a deeply rooted stance. When this happens he will be uprooted and knocked over. There are literally hundreds of combinations and levels of these two extremes, but they are all variations on a theme.

If the person's stance is too high and narrow—and he tries to resist instead of allowing himself to be moved—he will be tilted over in the direction of the force. This means his feet were too close together and his center of mass too high to resist the amount of force coming in. You will often see this when people list backward and run back as they try to reestablish their balance by getting their feet underneath them again. They are literally running backward to keep from falling. Just as often, however, when they try to reestablish structure in this position you will see them being slammed into the ground.

An interesting point to remember is that the human body can collapse to a point where it regains structure. Often it will collapse to a point where you could resist if you were still upright. Unfortunately, if you are bowled over, getting structure back as you are teetering on the edge of falling doesn't save you. It only allows for more power to be delivered into you. Put simply, you get structure back just in time for it to assist in knocking you over. Now the real bad news: getting structure back at this time will actually make you hit the ground harder.

If you are attacked while in too high and narrow a stance, it is easier and faster to throw a stalling structure instead of trying to drop down into a rooted, structured stance. Look at the timing of the latter: you are trying to build a fortress after the attack has already been launched. It is technically possible to do it, but if you aren't in just the right position, your structure will collapse. A reality check here: slapdash jobs usually have slapdash results; as such, the chances of your doing it wrong are greater than of doing it right.

But this is what people try to do instead of executing a fast, stalling structure between them and their attacker, which would enable the incoming force to be surfed until it begins to falter and is subject to manipulation. The nice thing about this is that you don't need a perfect structure to stop your opponent, but just enough to keep him at a distance that allows him to push you aside. The harder he pushes, the easier it is for you to surf his force.

You can tell the difference between someone who is being run backward and someone who is intentionally allowing his structure to be moved by an incoming force by what happens when the opponent stops pushing. Someone who is in balance and is letting his structure be pushed will stop when the incoming force stops. Someone who is being bowled over will have to take extra steps in order to get his feet back under him.

Using the strongest structural position of any block that you choose, have your partner push against it. Let him push you around the room. The structure keeps him at a fixed distance. Don't resist, just move with his pressure. Let him roll the boulder while you calmly tell him the myth of Sisyphus.

Once you have gotten to the point where you are easily moving with the force, start over. This time try to dig in, but do it wrong, intentionally mess up. In other words, take too high a stance, take the right leg position, but put your upper arm in the wrong place. Take the correct stance and limb position, but turn your hips too far or not far enough. By intentionally taking incorrect structural positions while attempting to resist, you will be bounced around like a pinball.

These flawed structures that you are intentionally creating are exactly what happens when someone attempts to throw up a fixed defense against a strong and overwhelming attack. Instead of using structure to stall the attack long enough to move, they attempt to stop it with incorrect structure and an incorrectly rooted position. That is why these attacks get through.

This is why I say, if faced with an unexpected attack, become a car in neutral. Get your structure (arms) up and let him push you. By rolling with it, he gets no closer. You can wait until his force has diminished enough before you pop the clutch. If, however, the attack has overwhelmed your structure to the point of falling, don't try to get it back. Go into tumbling mode.

I should point out something else: If you are surfing an incoming force, you don't have to have perfect position with your arms (structure). You can be close enough. Yes, there will be a little bowing and flexing, but because you are moving with the force instead of resisting it, you can be a little off position without its becoming a problem.

Earlier in this chapter I wrote the following: "As you will see, a block—the way most people do it—is the most ineffective means of defense. It's a move that, while it may save your butt, does not set you up for anything else even if done correctly. It needs to be considered an emergency defensive move, not your first option." But blocking and rolling with it must be in your "defensive toolbox."

In the sword-fighting world there is a man who has made a name for himself by insisting that edge-to-edge blocking didn't exist in medieval sword work. To say that this caused a controversy would be like saying that the *Titanic* sprang a small leak—a bit of an understatement. His original premise is that because blocks are slow and do not put you into a strategic position, they weren't used at that time. He has developed a sword-fighting art based on parries and counters and has many followers who preach his gospel.

I don't disagree with his premise that blocks are inferior to parries and counters. In fact, I agree. I disagree that blocks have no value and were not used. They have an incredibly important value in that *blocks, like body armor, cover your mistakes.*

You are not always going to get the first shot off, nor are you always going to be ready for it. You will sometimes get caught flat-footed. In fact, even in the middle of a screaming confrontation, the first attack often comes as a surprise. There is no bell that tells you to come out fighting. Usually, you know you are in a fight when the guy's fist crashes into your face.

Furthermore, there are a lot of times in a violent conflict in which things come out of nowhere and head at you at a high speed. These situations are exactly where blocks come in handy. When you are not in the position or have the time to do anything else, you have a choice: block or bleed.

People often don't have enough time to create the proper structure to stop an attack but that doesn't stop them from trying. In that case, they both block and bleed. This is why there is a legitimate distrust regarding the effectiveness of blocks. But it is distrust based on all the wrong reasons. Instead of dismissing blocking, you should avoid attempting to block without structure or movement, and in circumstances when something else would work better.

With a block and roll, you buy yourself time to do something else. There is very definitely a time to block, just as there are other times when it is better to do something else. Quite honestly, though, a block and roll lends itself very well to aikido-type solutions. As your opponent is running out of steam from pushing you, it is extremely easy to grab the attacking limb and accelerate its owner right into a wall. This is part of the reason I get so excited about the idea of someone really trying to hit me hard. The harder they attack, the easier it is for me to dribble them like a basketball. I do it by first using a block and roll, and next by hijacking all that incoming force they are feeding me; then, using all the energy they gave me, I throw them face first into a wall.

There is a reason why block and roll is here to stay.

When speaking of blocks and deflection it's vital to know the difference between a basic and a fundamental. These two terms are often confused because their first definitions are sometimes similar in abridged dictionaries. It isn't until you begin to read other definitions and other dictionaries that you will see a very important difference. What follows is a down-and-dirty summation of the difference you will find in a dictionary.

A *basic* is an introduction. A *fundamental* is a foundation.

A fundamental is a premise, idea, or fact that an entire system arises from and is based on. Put simply, a fundamental determines the shape of what arises from it, much as a foundation of a house dictates its layout.

A basic is how you introduce people you are teaching to the system. It is a beginning concept, often simplified to assist learning. For example, if you are trying to teach someone Tae Kwon Do, you first show them a basic punch. You don't show them how to do a jumping, spinning heel kick. If a fundamental is the foundation, a basic is the front door to enter the system.

The reason I mention this is that these terms are used interchangeably in many schools. Instructors stress "know your basics" when they should be saying "know your fundamentals." You practice basics so you can ingrain fundamentals. To do this after the introduction of basics, one needs to shift focus to perfecting the fundamentals through these basic moves. If you know to look for them, the fundamentals can be clearly seen in the basics. They are not, however, easily seen in advanced, complicated techniques. That is why you will see beginners and advanced students practicing the same moves in many traditional schools. The beginning student is working on the gross movement; advanced students focus on different aspects, making little tweaks and adjustments. I often tell students that a basic can be learned in five minutes, but fundamentals can take years to fully understand.

In schools that make no distinction between these two terms, people rush past the basics hoping to get to the "good stuff." When told they need to pay attention to the "basics," they dismiss the idea as too rudimentary, not realizing the difference between a fundamental and a basic.

In doing so, they ignore the fundamentals and do not ingrain them into their consciousness and reactions. Then they wonder why what they are trying to do falls apart in the ring, or, worse, doesn't work in a fight.

A block is a basic. It is a very good starting point, largely because, to a beginner, all attacks are unexpected and overwhelming.

Deflection, however, is a fundamental. It just looks like a block. Although it is it based on a block, it is much more than that, and you have to look in order to see the difference.

In most schools a block is designed to stop, push aside, or stall an incoming force. It does not necessarily put you into a good position to counterattack. You can still counterattack, but most of the time you cannot immediately deliver force into your opponent with your next move.

I want you to pay close attention to that "next move" part. Unless your attacker has politely stopped in the perfect location and range, the odds are that you have to reposition in order to deliver force. There is a big difference between your next move's being an attack and your preparing to attack.

EXTRA MOVEMENT WHILE PREPARING TO ATTACK

Block punch.

Clear arm/cock back.

Punch.

It may not seem like much, but when you have three seconds you don't want to waste two of them preparing to do something. The reason many people don't realize this is that they consider the movement that prepares the attack to be part of the actual attack. It isn't. What's worse, this preparation gives your opponent extra time to stop your attack when you finally get around to it.

Obviously, this preparation violates the rule of not using extra or unnecessary movement. Yet, since it generally happens so fast and always in front of an attack, we tend not to recognize it as a movement separate from the attack itself. Here's a really good rule of thumb: An attack is a motion that delivers force into your opponent and affects his ability to attack you. Any action that you execute prior to that attack is a setup action.

As you can see in the illustrations, there is an entire set of motions that are neither offensive nor defensive. They are preparatory to making an offensive move. While they look great for the camera, they are not fence. They have done nothing to keep your opponent from attacking again or to move you to a more strategic position. Their only purpose is to set up one punch. This kind of setup is extremely vulnerable to a second attack, which you can pretty well expect because you haven't moved out of his target area.

These extra steps take time and interrupt channeling force. They may take less than a second, but that extra movement is still there. This is why the idea of blocking is often sneered at by gurus of so-called deadly fighting arts—until a sucker punch pastes their face onto the wall because they didn't have time to do any of those fancy moves they preach.

Here is a very important rule: You practice blocks for when you are unexpectedly attacked or rudely surprised. You practice deflections, counters, and parries for when you are a little more in control of the situation and are working toward a strategic goal.

Here is an important concept for understanding the differences between blocking and deflecting. There are four options for moving:

1. You move
2. You don't move
3. You are moved
4. Or a combination of 1 & 3

Each option has its own set of dynamics. Each also has strengths and weaknesses, advantages and problems. In short, there is no generic *best way* or even *right way* that you *always do it*. You learn all four and use them appropriately.

Generally, the difference between a block and a deflection is based on (a) when you move and (b) who makes that move happen. In many cases, you block and are moved by the incoming force. You move after the force arrives.

For a deflection you will often use the same structure as for a block, but you have moved into a fence location where either your next move is a strike or the structure itself can be used as a strike. With a deflection, you move before the force arrives and by doing so redirect the incoming force.

Moving before or moving after the force arrives; moving or being moved. It may seem like splitting hairs, but you would be amazed at the important differences in the physics of these respective options.

What you are seeing in the following illustration is an example of deflection. The defender is initiating his body move-

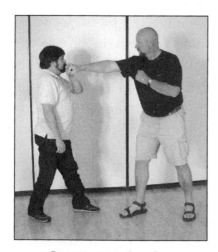

Incoming punch to face.

Hammerfist to groin.

ment as part of what most people would call a block. In this book, a block is what happens when you either don't move or are moved. A deflection is what happens when you start the body movement as a part of moving into fence. It's a seemingly small difference, but it is important.

This also is an example of moving into a position in which there is no need for prep time to change from a defensive to offensive move. In fact, these are different parts of a greater whole, not separate moves. The setup for the strike is accomplished by the movement; the same movement that has ruined his second attack. By moving his body when the attack was coming in, the defender has developed fence. This is a more basic—and easily seen—example of fence. The defender's movement is toward a location and body position where he doesn't have to waste time or motion setting up his attack. His next move is an attack.

Notice that now the attacker cannot initiate an effective second attack without inserting a setup move. He must stop, reorient, and then attack again.

This move is pure fence, something that both protects you and develops your attack potential. By moving into this position, the defender has made it necessary for the attacker to insert extra movement before he can attack again. Extra movement takes time and confronts him with a choice. He can abandon his setup and defend against the counteroffensive, or he can try to suck it up and keep on trying to set up his next attack.

The latter is not a good choice because you don't lightly soak up an effective counteroffense.

And there is no law that says the defender can't do the same thing again by moving into a new fence position after delivering the first counterattack. The defender can repeatedly move to a new fence position. Sure, the attacker might be able to soak up one fence-based counterattack, but how about five or six?

Sooner or later, the idea of *paying attention to incoming fire* is going to start looking real good to the attacker. When it does, his offense will falter.

Incoming punch.

Step in/deflect/strike.

Deflection becomes a strike/outside block.

Here the defender not only changes range in order to destroy the attacker's effectiveness, but positions himself close enough so that his deflection counters the incoming limb.

This deflects its force, rather the stopping it. He also has positioned himself in a range where his deflection serves as a blow.

The illustration is for demonstration purposes only. For that move to work, a parry would have to be deployed first. This would have cleared the path for the slower, heavier deflection, as well as given the defender a safe place to step. It is important, however, to individually illustrate the concept of a moving structure deflecting an incoming force.

I would also like to point out that, as shown in the illustration, a deflection can be used as a strike because it entails moving into the correct range. There is a grave misconception in the martial arts and defensive tactics world that a block can be used as a hit. Blocks don't make good strikes, but deflections can. In order to use a deflection as a strike, however, you must understand range, body movement, and structure. Notice though that I said "strike," not "hit." Hits reach out, impact a target, and then withdraw. A strike, however, has no such restriction. A strike inserts structure and gives you choices of action. Yes, you can withdraw the structure. Or you can press forward with it or you can leave it there to prevent your opponent from returning to the position you knocked him out of when you struck with your structure. Because it retracts, a hit does none of these.

The defender, by initiating his body movement before the hit arrives, turns his block into a deflection—even though he is using the same structure as a block. His moving mass and structure totally change the physics of what is happening. What is most important, however, is that by combining movement with a so-called block, he doesn't have to do as much of either.

Bob Orlando has a fabulous way of demonstrating the importance of combining movement with blocking to create deflection. He has a person throw three straight punches. The first he blocks. The second he dodges. Each of these movements must be done to an extreme in order to avoid being hit. On the third punch he does both, i.e., blocks and dodges. In doing so, he lessens the need for extremes with either. He can literally do half of each. By moving the proper direction his block turns into a deflection. Because he is moving out of the target area, he doesn't need to stop the force, but only deflect it.

Imagine you are throwing a straight punch to the nose. The first option shown below would move your punch. The second would avoid your punch. The third, however, would do both. That is a form of deflection. Get a partner and try this.

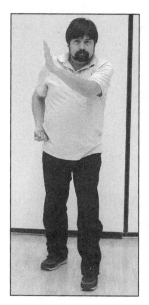  

Full block (inside with right hand).   *Dodge.*   *Deflect (inside with right hand).*

The third option puts the defender in a much better tactical position. From there he is able to both counter-attack immediately (look at his left hand) and defend against another attack. This is not necessarily true of the other two positions.

I would also like to point out that deflection is a matter of movement and angles, not of just rushing headlong into an opponent—even though that is what it might look like. An accomplished martial artist in a system that uses circles commented that his instructor's circles had become so small that they looked like straight lines. He said that the new generations of students weren't doing circles anymore, but straight lines, because that is what they thought they saw. There are many important lessons to be learned from that discussion.

What looks to the untrained eye like a headlong rush is quite often an intentional movement to a subtle angle. There are more directions in which one can move than straight in and to the "45." Training yourself to move along different angles is one of the "secrets" of deflection. Of course, one man's secret is another man's good-quality instruction. And good quality always outperforms secrets when things go sideways. So don't get too hung up on the secrets of a fighting style.

Several important points arise from this idea of moving on subtle angles. The first is that incoming energy deflects more easily off an angle. If your structure is moving on an angle, deflection is much easier. Second, deflection can come in many forms. You can move on one angle and block/parry from another. Or you can hold your structure up while moving along an angle. Or you can hold your limbs at an angle while moving in a straight line.

The third point is that, to an untrained eye, a subtle angle makes something look as if it is coming in straight. And that is what will get you successfully in. I often say that the attacks that hurt me the most weren't the ones I didn't see coming. They were the ones I saw and thought were something different. I countered for what I thought they were, and was seriously dismayed to discover that they were something else. Those moves really nailed me.

Look at it from your opponent's perspective: you coming in on a subtle angle looks as though you are coming straight in, and that is what your opponent will brace for. He's expecting to get hit head-on. But the physics that a subtle angle creates are very different. What's more, you often slip past his defenses because he thinks you are somewhere else. His block goes to the center. You, however, are an inch or so to the left of it. He's in the wrong place to stop you.

The fourth point is that subtle angles are instrumental for moving into fence, the place where you can hit him but he can't hit you. Moreover, he won't realize where you are heading until it is too late.

Fifth, the power of the deflection comes from being struck by a moving structure. Your structure has mass behind it. You can withstand a wind of 20 mph, but would you want to get hit by a car moving at the same speed? This is why deflection is so much more powerful than blocking.

Unfortunately, I am not able to delve more deeply into deflection. Different styles "block" differently. How they manifest deflection varies wildly. If I were to try to show how to create deflection in all the different styles, this book would turn into an encyclopedia. What I can say, however, is that any system you study has the necessary components for the understanding and effective application of both blocks and deflections.

What I can give you is an exercise to help you learn deflection. Go back to the heavy bag, with the Vs on the floor. The widest V should be on the 45.

Make the angles 45, 60, 75, and 90. Now pick any defensive handwork from your style (i.e., what you thought of as a "block" until I got hold of your definitions). It doesn't matter which handwork you choose. Start the bag swinging along the 90 line, step forward as it swings back, and block. Then step along the various angle lines and "block" the bag. What you are doing is a deflection.

I will warn you right up front that in the beginning you will get slammed into and knocked over by the bag. That's OK. In fact, pay close attention to those occurrences because they are showing you weaknesses in your structure and timing. If you get knocked ass over teakettle, obviously that isn't the place you want to be. Try moving to a new spot and doing it again, or check your structure.

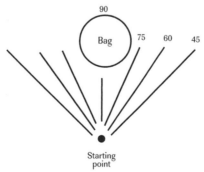

Stacked Vs, 45, 60, 75, 90.

This exercise will not necessarily teach you where to move when dealing with a human being. Only practicing with another human can do that. What it will do, however, is instill in you the ideas and fundamentals that you will need in order to figure out what works on an opponent.

- 9 -

Parrying and Countering

Battles are won by slaughter and maneuver.
The greater the general the more he contributes in maneuver,
the less he demands in slaughter.

—Winston Churchill

There is no consistent definition or use of terms anywhere. I have seen martial arts systems in which what I define as parries were called blocks, and others in which deflection was considered the result of parrying. In some, the only way to counter was by counterpunching. For many years I used the term *slap block* for what I now refer to as a parry. That was to differentiate slap blocks from heavier karate blocks. But in the schools where I learned them, they were simply referred to as blocks.

And if you think the subject is confused in martial arts circles, you ought to hear some of the debates that go on in fencing and sword-fighting circles—taken one notch up, these debates would be donnybrooks.

Again, not in an attempt to set an industry standard, but for the clarification of different ideas, I will define a parry as a fast, sharp blow against the side of or from behind an incoming force that causes it to veer off course. You literally slap it aside.

There is another way to create a parry, through a rotational movement, but that subject is worthy of a book itself. I will limit myself in this book to the more quickly learned and more easily applied fast-strike type of parry.

You can liken this to a beat in fencing or an *abiniko* in kali, where you slap your opponent's blade to the side in order to clear a path for your move. A beat, however, is usually a move that you initiate when his blade is stationary. A parry is made against an incoming attack.

In this definition a parry can have structure or can rely on speed alone. It can be done while moving or while stationary. The speed comes mostly from the arms zipping into position.

Imagine that you and your friend are slap boxing. The fast, light blows require fast "blocks." These actions are significantly different from what it takes to stop a full-on, heavily committed strike. Instead of using the same word to describe different actions, let's call one *parrying* and the other *blocking*.

Parries work best against fast attacks. But they often fail against heavier, more powerful attacks, just as blocks are often too slow to stop a fast, speed-based attack. This simple fact creates massive amounts of confusion when people use the word *block* to define both types of movement. Do you make your blocks effective against hard blows, or against fast strikes? No matter which way you go, you are going to get hit by the other half.

Or do you try to perfect a single move that supposedly does both? From my days of backyard mechanics, I remember a phrase we used about after-market parts that were supposed to work in different cars: "one size fits none."

This is why defining the difference between a parry and a block is so important. With two definitions you are not trapped between the devil and the deep blue sea. You have choices, and you know which works for what.

A parry creates a deflection of a fast incoming force. That which makes the incoming attack fast also makes it vulnerable to a quick parry. The faster his attack, the more vulnerable it is to being smacked off course.

Personally, if I have time, I prefer to do parries on the diagonal, coming in diagonally from behind. I do this instead of meeting the incoming blow perpendicular to its line of force. Instead of trying to get in front of the blow or trying to knock it far enough to the side to miss me, I come in from behind and push it past me.

I prefer this option for several reasons. They will be more clearly demonstrated if you experiment with the idea without moving. Even without body movement, you will get good results. When you combine these parries with body movement, you get great results. But first practice these elements in isolation, so that you can see how effective they are on their own before you blend them.

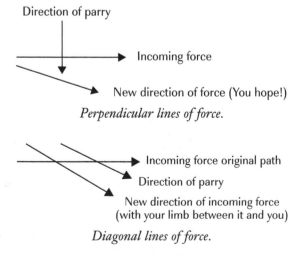

Direction of parry

Incoming force

New direction of force (You hope!)

Perpendicular lines of force.

Incoming force original path
Direction of parry
New direction of incoming force
(with your limb between it and you)

Diagonal lines of force.

To use a perpendicular parry and cause an incoming blow to veer off enough to miss, you must have very good timing and must hit it hard enough. You have to hit it soon enough and back far enough so that the deflection has time to take effect and make the blow miss you. Otherwise, all you do is move the blow from one side of your face to another. And you have to hit it hard enough so it veers off enough to miss you entirely, or again you will have just moved it to where you are going to get hit.

Unfortunately, in order to compensate for both hard enough parries and a lack of structure, many schools teach their students to parry and dodge. While this may sound like the same principles I have been talking about, what these schools are teaching is the student must literally throw himself to the side to avoid being hit. The problem with this is twofold. First, it is not fence. The student has thrown himself out into the boonies, from which it is difficult to launch a counteroffensive without having to do set ups and move into an attack position. Second, it gives the attacker time to regroup, reorient and set up his next attack. That means while you avoided being hit, you're right back to where you started nose to nose with someone attacking you.

Parrying hard enough to keep from getting hit may not sound like much of a problem, except that the line between "hard enough" and "too hard" is very thin. It is easy to overshoot and go too far out, leaving yourself open for the next attack.

When parrying diagonally this doesn't matter; in fact, the harder and faster you hit, the better the results will be. You never go farther out of line than the edge of your shoulder and that gives you both speed and structure.

My second reason for preferring a diagonal instead of a perpendicular line is that parrying really is a matter of time and space. An ideal parry must be out far enough that there is both time and space for the blow to miss you. With sufficient time and space, the parry can be a very light tap. However, the closer to your body that you intercept the incoming force, the harder and faster you must parry. What is a tap farther out must become a smash closer in. Unfortunately, most people try to do perpendicular parries much closer in, instead of farther out (near countering range) where they should be done.

There are several complications to perpendicular parrying. One, people tend to tense up when they try to do things hard. Tight muscles are slow muscles, which lessen your chance of getting into position in time. Two, parrying perpendicularly requires much better timing and speed than does diagonal parrying. If off, you're going to get hit. Three, people often turn their bodies in order to hit hard enough to deflect the blow. This not only turns them away from their opponent, so they cannot effectively counterattack with their next move, but, quite frankly, turns a parry into an aggressive block—with all the problems associated with hitting with your block. Four, most people try to do a perpendicular parry too close to their own chest.

Get a chest protector and a partner and try this drill. Have your partner throw a straight punch toward your covered chest. With either hand, reach out and "slap" his elbow. Don't focus on his fist; aim for points close to the elbow. Slap perpendicular to your chest. Play with this for a while, until you're able to keep most blows from landing or your partner thinks his arm is going to fall off. This is a painful exercise for him.

Now try to parry closer to your body. Try to slap his fist as it is coming toward you. For your partner this will be payback for what you did to his arm. It also demonstrates why you are wearing a chest protector: you will get hit a lot. In time, you will find that the number of hits decreases. When that happens, see what position you have ended up in. The odds are that you will have twisted and dodged into positions that do not face your partner. This is how you keep from getting hit when you are working this close to him.

If you have moved into this position against a faster boxing jab, you are not where your very next move can be an attack. You will have to set up your counterattack or, at least, spend extra time traveling to get into position for it, because you are way out in the boonies. You will have unwittingly fallen into another type of flawed training: the automatic twist to compensate for a weak parry. This is close cousin to automatically throwing yourself to the side to avoid being hit. Although both prevent you from being hit, what they don't do is prevent you from being hit *and* put you into a superior tactical position (fence). As I said earlier, this doesn't matter much in a sports context, but it's critical in a violent situation.

Another problem is that this has turned into more of a typical block than a parry. Granted that turning your body this way while blocking close in is not a problem against a heavy, overcommitted attack. In fact, blocking this way against such an attack puts you in a perfect position to counterattack because you deflect your opponent instead of stopping him. When this happens, he rushes right in front of you. Not only do you have him in range, but he is also likely to be off balance.

A perpendicular parry, however, is a problem against the lightning-fast delivery and machine-gun repetition of boxing punches—or any attack that will not stumble forward if your face is not there to stop it. You don't want to turn to the side against such an attacker. In avoiding one punch, you are setting yourself up to take two or three others.

My third reason for preferring diagonal to perpendicular parries is that they are more natural. Unless you move in a very specific way to keep your hands close to your body, your arms tend to swing out and back as you raise them to your face. Try it. Stand with your hands at your sides and then swing them up to your face. This is a very natural movement. You will notice that around your chest, your hands will be the farthest point away from you in a natural arc. Your hands go out and then come back in because of the length of your forearms.

You have wonderful tool by design. Use it.

Just by swinging your hands in a natural manner to defend your face, you give yourself the distance that a parry needs. Your hands are in a position to affect his elbow, and (when you think about it, it's rather obvious) by extension, his fist. That fist is connected to his elbow. Where the elbow goes, the fist will follow.

Unfortunately, many people attempt to either tuck their elbows in or "chicken wing" them out in order to get their hands in close to parry the fist. They negate this wonderful design feature of the human body. You can bring your hands to your face while keeping your hands close to your chest, but your elbows will take one of these two unacceptable positions.

My fourth reason for preferring diagonal parries is that they are strikes, not hits. That is to say they leave a structure between my attacker and me. This structure serves as a shield to prevent him from closing with me. In addition, if it turns out his attack is too strong, that structure can turn from a parry into a block (block and roll).

My fifth reason for preferring to come in diagonally with a parry is that if I come straight in from the side on his attack, I have to hit to deflect, and it all has to be done in one spot. By coming in from behind, my parry becomes a guide. I don't knock the blow aside, but direct it where I want it to go.

Usually, where I want it to go is right into a trap.

The nasty things that you can do by coming in on a diagonal from behind are legion. To begin with, have you ever been running and had someone push you from behind? Have you ever been tackled from the side while running? Which took more force to put you down? It was being tackled from the side. This method of parrying is the same idea, but you do it to his blow. By parrying this way, you are getting both the ease and effect of hitting from behind, plus the extra damage of hitting from the side—but without the work. Hitting from behind takes less force to make everything go kaput. Another nasty trick lies in the fact that you are destroying his structure and hyper-extending his limb. His structure is designed to deliver and resist force in specific directions. It isn't designed to resist being hit from behind. On top of everything else, by throwing in the slightest degree of diagonal, you not only make it harder for him to retract quickly, but easier for you to grab that same limb.

I would like you to pick up a small object and toss it back and forth, hand to hand. Pretty easy to catch it, isn't it? With a little bit of practice you can do the same thing with his incoming blow. Your parry guides his incoming blow into your other hand, which is waiting to catch it.

And once you have that arm, you not only have leverage, but a direct line to his vertical axis. Do with it what you will, because those are incident-stopping conditions. They are exactly the circumstances you need in order to put an immediate stop to the fight.

The following illustrations show you the basic angles and end positions that I recommend you practice. Where the X crosses should be about chest height. Practice moving your arms along this line in order to end up in the positions shown.

When you do this, don't focus on moving your hands down these lines, instead focus on your forearms. When you watch your forearms instead of your hands, you will see an interesting effect. Your forearms act as windshield wipers. They "wipe" a

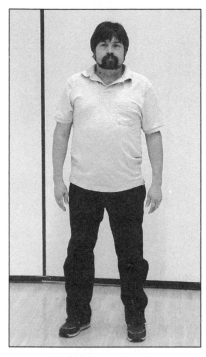

Hands down by side.

Cross body.

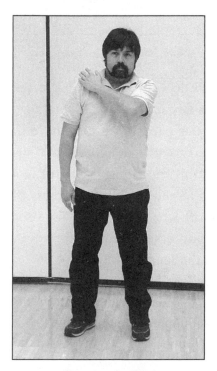

Opposite shoulder.

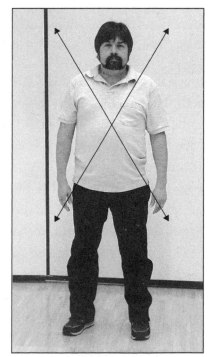

"X" pattern.

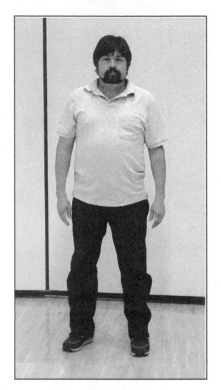 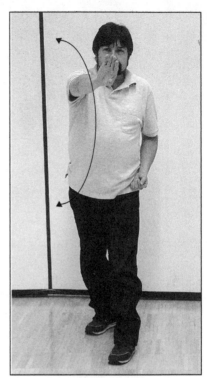

Hands down by side. *Same concept but on same side.*

much larger part of the angle than do your hands. That is exactly what you want. By covering a larger area, you do not have to be exact in the placement of your parry. You don't have to parry with your hand; you can parry with your forearm. This also renders the exact location of his incoming punch of less importance. Your hand is only so large, as is the thickness of his arm. If you are a few inches off when parrying with your hands, you will get hit. When using your forearms, however, the length of your forearm meets the length of his.

Not only is that more likely to happen, but it makes where they meet less important. If you are going to guide his arm aside, it doesn't matter much where your limbs meet, but where they meet is very important if you try to *knock* his arm aside.

There are many ways to do this drill, but I recommend that first you practice it in front of a full-length mirror. Don't watch yourself doing the parries, instead watch what the parries are doing. That is a very subtle, but important, difference. If you think of the angles as sheets of fogged glass that you are wiping with your coat sleeve, you will notice that you are standing behind them. Nothing coming at you from that direction can get through without first going through this sheet of glass. Instead of thinking about shooting a bullet or throwing a rock through glass, think about what happens to a person who crashes through a plate-glass window: he gets torn up.[1]

Doing this drill in front of a mirror makes sure that your "wiping" keeps you behind the sheet of glass. Your body is behind the wipe. If you reach too far, you leave yourself exposed on the same side. If you don't go far enough with your wipe, you leave yourself open on the other side. Practice these wiping actions by moving your elbow to various positions. You will be able to see in the mirror that some positions leave parts of you exposed and vulnerable to attack. The position that gives you the most coverage is the right position for you.

When you have gained some confidence with using your forearms as fast windshield wipers, you can go back to using your hands. I prefer trying to hit the incoming blow with the fleshy part, where my palm meets my wrist. It is low enough that I can protect my fingers, but high enough to be near the part of my limb that is moving fastest. Wrist flexing also gives

---

1. Thinking of angles as 3-D constructs instead of mere lines in the air can—and will—have a profound effect on your understanding of angles. The more you play with this idea, the more profound are its implications.

you more power because of added movement. Don't try this, however, until you have done a good job of covering the angles with your forearms. This allows you to parry on the right diagonal instead of just trying to slap the blow aside perpendicularly. This tends to happen if you go too fast without first ingraining the angle.

Once you have these motions down, try combining them with body movement. Yes, until now I have told you to do these exercises without stepping into fence, so that you could learn the importance of angles and parries.

At first, just transfer your weight while parrying. When you are comfortable with moving and parrying at the same time, go back to the stacked Vs and the swinging bag. Move down the angles while parrying. You will be amazed at how you can make that bag dance just by slapping it. It moves where you want it to, and you move out of its way.

I often refer to parrying as "throwing salt over your shoulder." It is an old superstition that you throw a pinch of salt over your shoulder to ward off bad luck. It is amazing how fast and easy it is to avoid an attack with a parry as you move into fence position.

Things get really sexy when you start combining parries with counters.

A counter is, by its nature, a checking move. I mean this not only in the hockey sense, but in the chess sense. You force your opponent into a position where he must make his next move in an attempt to save himself. (Not that he will succeed, because while his next move is trying to escape your coup de grace, you next move is . . . well . . . a coup de grace.) In this chess game, you can not only check the king, but take him, too.

One of the defining elements of a counter is that it happens "way over there." A parry goes out and comes back. A counter goes out, way out. In fact, the farther out, the more effective the counter is. What's more, it does all its dirty work in his yard.

There are several levels of counters. The most basic is when you just reach out and slam into the person's shoulder as he tries to punch. Some folks call this a stop hit, check, or stop check. While this keeps you from being struck with that particular punch, it doesn't really do anything to keep another one from pasting your face all over the wall—especially if the guy knows how to rebound off incoming energy. Feed me or any of my friends a stop hit, and we'll feed it right back to you from the other side. (Remember block and roll? Same principle, different attitude.)

Another form is the counterpunch. Simply stated, as he takes the outside, you take the inside. The secret to counterpunching, however, is subtle movement. You move to a place where his blow can't reach you, but yours can reach him. If you attempt to counterpunch without moving, you will discover who has longer arms. If you move into subtle fence position, it doesn't matter whose arms are longer. You will hit, he won't. And your hit will keep him from changing directions and hitting you because your structure is in the way.

Another type of counter is what I call the "pebbles in front of a skateboard" approach. Simply stated, this involves your inserting a structure that is not fully in his path, but enough to cause his force to veer off. Instead of attempting to stop all of his force, you stall a small part of it. It is this stalling of one part that makes the whole spin out of control. This is why I liken it to a pebble and a skateboard. There are four wheels on a skateboard, but it only takes one of them jamming—just for a second—for the momentum to go spinning off in other directions. Remember, momentum is a force. It doesn't suddenly stop because something is slowing up. What it does do, however, is change directions, as anyone who has ever flown off a skateboard can tell you. By the way, you don't fly straight off in a skateboard-vs.-pebble situation. You are thrown forward and down. The direction your mass is heading changes because of that small rock, and its friction against the earth. The direction change can be small or large, but it always occurs when a portion of mass in movement is stalled.

Counters like this tend to use the same angles as parries. Instead of moving out and back, they tend to keep moving out. For many different reasons, it is important to move back and forth along the lines that I described. I will, however, point out something. With proper use of these angles, your limbs become the source of deflection for his incoming force. It doesn't matter if you are parrying, countering, or deflecting. If you move in the right way, you bend his force to your will.

The key word here is *deflection*. You will feel very little force when you are in the correct structure and moving along the correct angle. In fact, like punching incorrectly, being in the wrong place will make you feel as if you are accomplishing more. Like range, proper angles are a matter of inches. When you find the correct location, it will seem as if your attacker missed because it took so little work on your part.

From a professional use-of-force perspective (e.g., control tactics), there is another form of countering. While the others are small rock slides that herald a coming avalanche, this type starts as an avalanche. The entire mountainside lands on your opponent all at once. In this kind of counter you extend a triangular structure and rush forward. Whether you call this a wedge, snowplow, spear, hacksaw, or flying V, the idea is the same. You create a wedge-shaped structure and charge forward. It is this angled structure running into the person that causes him to spin, twist, lose his balance, or otherwise destroy the structure and orientation that he is basing his threat on.

As a basic, I don't have a problem with this idea. It works because it utilizes body movement, structure, and a kamikaze form of range. It is like getting hit by a train with a cow catcher on the front . . . and you are the cow. What I have a problem with is how often it can—and will—knock the guy out of your control range. You send him reeling and have to chase after him. That means you have to endanger yourself again when reentering to take control.

In my mind, a more effective manifestation—effective in this case meaning that you don't get hit as much—is to use a counter to *clear a path* where you want to go. This allows you to safely move into position to put him down and stop his aggression. I liken this to a snowplow that cuts a path that enables you to drive to work. In order to get to work, you need a cleared road.

This requires a kind of "collapsing counter," which doesn't go out and then come back so much as it goes out and you catch up to it. Extend your arm and then step up. As you do so, fold your arm so that your chest touches your hand. That is distinctly different from shooting your hand out and then bringing it back. A collapsing counter not only deflects his incoming force, but keeps him from moving back into position to attack. And it does this while you move into a much better attack position, one that gives you range, body movement, and structure. In other words, you can use a counter to develop fence.

Again let me stress that the secret to this kind of counter isn't that it goes out and then comes back; that would be a parry. This counter goes out, and then you catch up.

Shoulder touch.

Step in/arm collapse.

I would like to point out that this counter can—and often does—serve as a strike. After you ring his chimes, as you move into position your arm collapses. It creates both a shield and a check against his turning and reorienting on you. And here is where it gets really sweet: it more than likely sets up for another hit, too.

Attempt at the very least to move behind his elbow. It is better still to move behind his shoulder. It is interesting to note that even though you are folding your structure, there is enough force being passed into him that it can and will speed the spinning/structure-breaking effect you have created with your strike.

Now that we have looked at each of these elements individually, I want you to realize that they can and do combine—and beautifully. It is that combination that clears your way to move into fence.

I want you to consider the importance of what I just said. All of these are designed not necessarily to stop his attack from reaching you, but to stall or deflect it while you move somewhere else—to a location where you can attack him, but he cannot attack you.

I would like to describe one of my favorite combinations of parrying, countering, and deflecting. There are many reasons for my liking this type of move. Once you experiment with it a bit, I think you will begin to see the possibilities, as well.

Parry.

Deflect/counter.

Strike.

View from other side.

It is important to consider this not as three moves, but as one move with three parts. The combination creates a multi-layered clearing action that allows you to safely move into attack position against a wide variety of attacks.

I say this because against a heavy attack the fast parry will cause the attack to veer enough so that you can get your slower, but structured, deflection/block/counter up without interference. If it is a fast blow the parry serves to deflect it, while the counter works as either a hit or a deflecting action to get him moving off line. Depending on which angle you take, your heavier move will either hit or counter—perhaps both—his second attack as you move.

When I show this as a closing move I am frequently asked whether it's two steps or one long step to get into this position. The answer is yes. It can be either of these, or a combination of a longer step and a shorter one. It doesn't matter; they all work. It depends on what you are most comfortable with and can do the quickest.

Go back to the swinging heavy bag and experiment with entering this way. Remember to move along the angles of the stacked Vs. Pay close attention to the multilayered nature of this move. No single aspect does everything, so don't try to make it all depend on one. It is the combination that will clear your pathway. As you are working the bag, watch how this technique will open avenues for you to move in. When you see such an opening, move there.

This is the first part of the exercise. Once you can easily "dance the bag" in this manner, to a point that you are making minimal movement while the bag is flying to the end of its chain, it is time to add attacks. You will notice by doing this exercise that you are constantly moving into the ranges of various attacks you have practiced. Go ahead and use them. Practice attacking a moving target with range, body movement, and structure. Using the bag, do this as hard and as fast as you can without sacrificing the Big 3.

Before you move on to the third part of this exercise, I want to discuss safety issues. For the record, I do not agree with the idea of *pulling your punches*, nor do I suggest that you try to hit to the surface of your partner's gi. My reasoning is that I feel this destroys rather than enhances a person's concept of range and proper body movement. Without extensive training in range, it is hard for someone to be able to correctly judge where to make a light hit. You are likely to goof and accidentally hit your partner harder than you wanted to. Furthermore, training yourself to pull your punches is training yourself in all kinds of bad habits. It also runs the risk of your sparring partner's moving unexpectedly and walking into your attack.

The way I train people to practice encourages correct body movement, range, and structure. In other words, if that puppy were to land, it would hurt bad. However, when you come in with the attack, you relax your "attacking" limb the second you feel contact. When you feel the touch, you literally let your arm become a noodle. By doing this you break your structure, intentionally. Instead of being hit by a freight train, your partner is hit by a noodle thrown from that train.

My reason for training people to do this is that it still allows them to work the concepts of body movement, range, and structure into everything they do. In time you will also learn it is a great way to control the level of force you apply in any type of move. With this idea you can easily scale the same tactics to work under a wide variety of circumstances. You use the same principles to control drunken Uncle Albert at a family reunion or to end an attack during a road rage incident. It is you controlling your structure that determines how much damage you do.

And while there is a chance that under the stress of a live-fire situation people will revert to this training, there is a compensating factor. Under the same stress a person's sense of proportion and distance is distorted, as are his reflexes. This makes it very likely that the person will overshoot and still deliver force into his opponent, even if he inappropriately breaks his structure in combat.

You can practice breaking your structure by stepping into range with the heavy bag and then going noodle-armed when you make contact. Unlike when you block and deflect, start with the bag stationary when you work with breaking structure. Work your way up to doing it against a moving target. In time, start practicing when to break your structure and how fast to relax. After working so hard to create structure, intentionally breaking it offers a shocking example of how important it is. You can experiment with varying degrees of power delivery by playing with the time at which you break your structure. Once you can break structure, move on to the third phase of the countering/parrying/deflecting exercise.

Have a partner come in with one-step attacks. No matter what kind of punch he throws, you clear the path and move into attack position, then attack. For this exercise you simply move into position and launch a single attack. If you can work an attack in during your parry/counter/deflection, that makes two attacks.

Having said this about breaking your structure, I still recommend that you practice with a partner who is wearing safety equipment. You shouldn't wear gloves, but he should wear protective gear. Also remember that your attacks, accelerations, and hip turns should come near the end of the weight transfer.

When doing these exercises, it will also help to have an informed third party watching. By "informed" I mean someone who has read this book and is familiar with its concepts. He will be able to see actions that the participants are not aware they are doing. As such, he can comment on issues such as trying to move before you have cleared the path, leaning back and destroying your structure to avoid being hit, and many other problems that can arise until you learn to have faith in these moves.

In time you will find that clearing the path for where you want to go becomes an automatic priority. You won't even think about blocking; you will just move his attack to the side and zip to where you want to be. Do you move it with a block, a counter, a parry, or a deflection? It doesn't matter. You can use any one of them or any combination of them. What matters is that you meet the building code of moving.

– 10 –

Reconsidering What You Already Know

To ensure obtaining an objective, one should have alternate objectives.

An attack that converges on one point should threaten, and be able to diverge against another.

Only by this flexibility of aim can strategy be attuned to the uncertainty of war.

—Sir Basil H. Liddel-Hart

Dai-sifu Ark Wong used to say, "If it isn't over in three moves, step back and see what you are doing wrong." He often told my sifu, Alex Hulub, that, and my teacher repeatedly told it to me. It is a training goal and a fighting standard to work toward; one that I now pass on to you.

That simple rule has saved not only my bacon, but my life, many times. I heard it a lot while training. Twenty years later my sifu still reminded me of it. I tell you this because that rule was literally jackhammered into my awareness. It was a foundation of my fighting skill, and it is a fundamental of effective offense. Unfortunately, I cannot grind this concept into your head as it was ground into mine. You must do that yourself.

This rule establishes your priorities and guides your strategy. Everything you do will be aimed at achieving this goal. If you ever lose sight of this concept, you will lose your way toward effective offense.

Achieving this goal is not through doing three moves very hard and fast. In fact, when you attempt to do it this way, you usually end up knocking your opponent out of range and have to start over again.

The way to easily implement this strategy is by doing things that have multiple effects. Instead of doing three separate techniques, do one move that has three results. Think about the math for a second; it increases incrementally when you operate in this manner. If you do three things, the result is nine. "Over in three" is a whole lot less intimidating when your three equals nine the way someone else does it.

To achieve this *increase of effect*, however, it is necessary to think outside the box. And that means a lot of skull sweat and experimentation on your part. Nobody can conveniently hand you a system that does this for you. If you think they can, you'll soon realize that the only thing they have given you is a different box. You have to find what works best for you. What offensive concepts do you naturally gravitate toward? Which of them do you do best? Those are the ones you need to have in your arsenal. The trick is to know all the things those moves can be.

A punch is a punch, until it is something else. But in order to use it as something else, you have to learn to look at it in different ways. You have to understand the contributing factors that can either triple your effectiveness or rob you of the same. Things such as the angle you come in on, the way you move, and what you do with your other hand can have overwhelming effects on how well your offenses work. This is why I have elaborated on the components of effective offense. Not until you can separate them can you begin to see what else they can be and how they can be combined to create different reactions.

The same hand motion—when done with different body movements—will have radically different results.

So will the same move coming in on a different angle and at a different target. Do you want spectacular results? Try doing a simple technique while holding onto and pulling your opponent off-balance with your other hand! What was a simple hit immediately turns into a structure-destroying, reorienting setup for a throw. One move, three results.

In order to utilize this, however, you must pay attention to what you are doing and what effect it is having against an opponent. This means that you cannot *unconsciously* move in a preset and automatic fashion, as so many so-called experts advocate. You have to think about it while in training. In time, yes, the moves will become nearly subconscious. You will see the opportunity and react without even having to think about it. But before that happens, there is a conscious awareness of what it takes to move your body to achieve an end. That means establishing through training (1) coherent body movement and (2) the insertion of components necessary to achieve that end.

Unfortunately, most people are trained that a particular combination of body and hand motions is the "right" way to move. The problem with this training method is that the hand and the body motion become forever linked in this particular fashion. A punch literally becomes a punch forever. This pattern becomes so ingrained that the person cannot functionally move in any other way.[1]

---

1. If you have ever seen a hard stylist trying to learn a soft style, you will understand exactly what I mean. The way the two styles move is entirely different. Once ingrained, a style's body movement can be a difficult habit to break.

Intellectually, you may understand that a move may become something else. But your puppy brain is not intellectual, and in a crisis situation that is what is steering the boat. If for fifteen years you have trained your puppy brain to consider a certain move a punch in a live-fire situation, that is what it knows and will do.

This is why I disagree with the concept of *bunkai*, at least the way it is currently taught. In Western martial arts circles bunkai is often interpreted as a dogmatic application. Another fad in interpretation is it is the secret fighting moves hidden within the techniques. This latter interpretation is considered an advanced concept, as in, "after fifteen years of thinking that this is a punch, it is suddenly revealed as really a throw."

My complaint obviously isn't about the idea that a hand movement can have a totally different result. You betcha that it can be a hit, block, counter, and throw. All you have to do is be able to use it as such. My complaint is that the idea of bunkai is taught at the black-belt level and not as a white-belt fundamental. As such, to the puppy brain that move is forever nothing more than a punch.

When it comes to effective offense, I will forever be thankful for the time I spent studying Chinese systems. Not only did they open my eyes to the differences between wushu and gung fu (in other words, what the martial arts are about other than just fighting), but they also freed me from the *impact rut*.

For many years I was seriously confused when I heard people in the martial arts state that kung fu didn't work. The reason for my confusion is that I was using it all the time in live-fire situations . . . and with sterling results, thank you very much. Yet here were high-ranking, big-name martial artists with more full-contact tournament wins than you could throw a tonfa at, who were saying that—in their experience—these systems didn't do well at all. These were casual conversations over beers. I had never seen them compete and they had never seen me fight, but this point I encountered again and again.

Years later I was talking with my old sifu about this, and he gave me a piece of the puzzle. "This stuff is just dirty street-fighting," he said. "If we did it in a tournament, they'd throw us out."

He was right. The clawing, biting, ripping, gouging, slapping, grabbing, and twisting—in addition to hitting—that I was doing in live-fire situations would have gotten me immediately disqualified. It would be several years more before I came to a fuller realization about this issue, one that explains how both sides were right and sheds light on the deeper implications of the idea.

Remember how I talked about *limited-offense* situations? These are situations in which the types of offense are controlled and rules are in place about what you can and cannot do. Well, there's the crux of the matter. The stuff I was doing was designed to effectively operate in either unlimited- or total-offense situations. As such, about 75 percent of what I was doing was not allowed in tournaments. As a result a significant portion of my time in sparring matches was spent stopping myself from doing those things.

The tournament fighters were specifically trained in what was allowed. That was their area of specialization. They didn't have to stop themselves from using techniques. Everything they had available was approved, and they were trained to deploy it with lightning speed and no hesitation or second thoughts.

No wonder that the guys I spoke with regularly defeated kung fu practitioners in limited-offense situations. That's like putting a sprinter up against a cross-country runner in the 50-yard dash. The cross-country runner is going to lose.

Most limited-offense situations revolve around what I call *impact fighting*, in which the opponents literally focus only on hitting each other.

There is a reason for this. The way that they hit each other in sports is designed to minimize the damage. Furthermore, the human body, by design, can handle impacts better from the front. Toe-to-toe sports contests are limited to engaging in ways in which we are best suited to handle force.

It is not that they aren't hitting hard; they are. What has been removed, however, are other aspects, which would cause these same hits to be devastating. The rules and referees are present to keep these aspects from creeping in because they would result in serious injury.

Want some examples of these banned aspects? Head butts. Sweeping the opponent's support leg. Pulling his weight onto a leg in order to *weight* it, then kicking that leg. Trapping him against a *base* and then hitting him. Hyperextending his arm and then hitting it. Twisting the limb as you hyperextend it and then shattering it. These are just a few moves that will cause serious injury by making impacts far more destructive. What I want to point out is that these aspects are still present in many Chinese-influenced systems, as well as in some Filipino, Indonesian, and Malaysian systems.

The resulting mind-set is that people tend to forget that there are other ways to attack—or, more important, that aspects removed from sport training even exist. They train their puppy brains to react in very focused and narrow SOPs (standard operating procedures). The best reactions that their puppy brain knows are *intentionally dumbed-down techniques* designed not to hurt a training partner or fellow tournament player. Unfortunately, the guy coming at you in a live-fire situation is not your friend, and you need to stop him. That means doing something to damage him enough to make him stop.

People trained in tailored-for-safety techniques are at a loss when they encounter something different. They don't think about attacking another way, much less about having an effective response to such attacks. This point was ferociously made in the first Ultimate Fighting Championship, in which trained impact-style fighters were creamed by grapplers. The rules that prevented clinching, grabbing, and tackling in the former's limited-offense impact competitions did not apply. They could do nothing to keep from being taken down to the ground by grapplers. Until other participants shifted their training focus from solely striking to include grappling, the Gracies ruled that ring.

Many people used the trends in the UFC to define new and wider ways of training. This is a good thing—to a point. I am a strong advocate of cross-training. Nonetheless, I would like to bring up a very, very important fact: Even the UFC, Pancrase, K-1, and all the other no-holds-barred events are *limited-offense situations*. The participants are not trying to kill, or even to hurt, each other. You will notice that the term *no holds barred* is not the same as "no techniques barred"—all kinds of moves are not allowed. There have to be exclusions. Otherwise it wouldn't be a sport; it would be a slaughter.

But let's look at less extreme sports. It is easy to see that how they attack and what is allowed is restricted primarily to (a) striking, and (b) striking without the nasty aspects I mentioned earlier. As such, it is very much a limited-offense situation, designed to minimize damage to participants. The result is that people have developed blinders; they don't know this stuff exists. They overemphasize impacts, without putting in those forbidden aspects.

The good news is that this also tends to apply to the guy you are facing.

The odds are that all he really knows is to hit. This means that in a limited-offense situation, you stand a very good chance of being attacked only with blows. That is the strategy that most people base their attacks on. *And if you train for what happens most, you will be able to handle most of what happens.*

Grappling hasn't exactly hit the streets. Most of the people that you will confront will not be trained in submission fighting. There is a good reason for this. Submission fighting works very well under limited-offense circumstances—especially when you are attempting to control an opponent without harming him. If it is your job to regularly control violent people without injuring them, then yes you must be trained in submission fighting. In the same vein, if there is even the slightest chance that you will be called upon to sit on a drunken friend or out-of-control family member, then submission fighting is important to know. But it is not a safe strategy to attempt in an unlimited-offense situation. It is definitely not something you want to try to use against a total offense.

In other words, if the dude (or worse yet, dudes) is out to hurt you, don't do it. The ground is the last place you want to be in an unlimited- or total-offense situation.

That does not mean that key elements cannot be taken from grappling and applied in these situations, however. In many cases grappling concepts can be applied to moves you normally associate with impact attacks. This means that you can do them standing up in order to put him down.

Here's an example. One of the formulas that I have heard for throws is "enter, break, throw." It's a good summation of what you have to do. Those are the building codes that you have to meet. Move into position, break his balance, and then

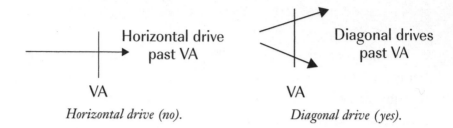

Horizontal drive (no).   Diagonal drive (yes).

throw him. So how do you do the same with an impact? We've already discussed the idea that punching six inches beyond his back is not an impact, but a drive attack. If you try to hit this way when he isn't charging full-bore or in a deep stance, the chances are good that he's going to go backward. That doesn't mean, however, that it isn't a valid way to attack.

Here is a simple example of putting in lost aspects that make effective offense. Just changing the angle of what was an ineffective punch turns it into an extremely effective uprooting, off-balancing, gravity-enhanced, driving blow. It does not depend on his stance in order to be effective. In fact, different stances cause different things to hurt worse when this bad boy connects.

Correct body movement and structure help achieve this drive. Keep your elbows down to prevent structural collapse, and move your body not only forward, but up. This gives your body the same diagonal direction when you transfer your weight. This means that your momentum is moving the same way. If you are going to experiment with this, make sure that your partner is wearing a hogue. It helps to have a third party watch, to make sure that your body is moving diagonally, instead of just straight ahead.

My point is that this kind of drive breaks his balance and structure and sets up either a throw or a takedown. Before you deliver this kind of drive, you need to have your other hand in place to pull him over. Otherwise, you won't be in position to exploit the reaction that you create, and he will regain balance and structure.

Effective offense is like running the table in pool. Each shot not only puts balls in pockets, but sets up your next shot. This is why you must learn to do things like putting your other hand out to pull, trap, off-balance, or twist him.

Slavo Gozdznik of the International Police Defensive Tactics Association has come up with the term *instinctive body reaction* (IBR). He contends that if you effectively apply force to a person, *something* will happen. It is up to you to exploit that reaction. The reason that I prefer Slavo's version over other, similar ideas is that IBR does not attempt to predict exactly what will happen, only that something will happen. It gives you a common range of reactions to look for, a way to recognize their significance, and stresses the importance of being where you need to be to make use of it.

While lecturing with Slavo in Sweden, I demonstrated this idea with an eye slap on two people. The first, a traditionally trained martial artist, reeled away with loud cries of pain. The head of the second person (who, it turned out, was a member of the prime minister's bodyguard) rocked back, then immediately snapped back, with a very dangerous gleam in his eye. I stopped the class and asked which was the real IBR. The class overwhelmingly identified the martial artist's reaction. "Wrong," I said, "they both were." The same blow, the same force, had totally different results. But both were direct results of the blow.

The challenge to the participants of that seminar was to learn how not to let that opportunity slip away. Unfortunately, most of them had not been trained to create fence, and as such were not in a position to exploit whatever IBR they created. The other person managed to recover before they could make something more out of it. Then they had to start the whole process over again.

I liken this to stepping through magical glass doors. These glass doors are not only locked, but magically repair themselves a second after they are broken. You have to break them and then step through before they mend themselves. Unfortunately, many people are too far back to be able to jump through after they break the glass.

The idea of putting in lost aspects is like having a rock big enough to allow you to shatter the glass. The idea of fence is putting yourself in a position where you can step through the broken glass door in time.

In other words, you have to be in the position to exploit whatever IBR you create. Otherwise he will react, but also will regroup before you can do anything with that reaction. You gain the ability to do this through understanding range and fence. You are able to create large IBRs by knowing how to apply the lost aspects of offense.

~ 11 ~

Regaining Lost Aspects

Strategy is the art of making use of time and space.
I am less concerned about the latter than the former.
Space we can recover, lost time never.

—Napoleon Bonaparte

If you look at them from a purely pragmatic point of view, many of the lost aspects really are time-saving devices. They give you extra time and steal it from your opponent. Instead of attacking you, he has to spend his time dealing with problems you create. And unfortunately for him, you just keep on stacking them up.

Fence alone will keep him from being able to immediately attack you again. It is the other things you do that will keep him from ever fixing that problem. I liken good offense to bureaucratic hell. You keep piling more and more red tape in front of him, keeping him from doing anything but dealing with the problems you create. Eventually, those problems will become overwhelming. His project of attacking you gets lost in the bureaucratic channels.

Consider the significance of what I just said. There is a major difference between an attack strategy that overwhelms your opponent and one that nitpicks him to death. Quite often, the reason that overwhelming offenses fail is that the person trying to do them has not done anything to prevent a counterattack. When that happens, the two offenses are likely to clash and stall. The nitpicking bureaucracy is like fighting a swarm of bees. Countless little things are going wrong, each one minor in itself, but collectively enough to ensure that his counteroffensive is never launched.

In the meantime you are landing on him like a ton of bricks.

Let me state right up front that causing pain is not a priority. When I said that each of your moves should do three things, I wasn't even including "inflict pain" on that list. Pain is a byproduct of other, more important factors. I say this because among those who commonly use violence to get what they want are a large number of people who have a very high tolerance for pain. If you are expecting pain to stop these people—or even slow them down—you are in for a rude surprise. In fact, you had better realize that there are a lot of people out there who, if you hurt them, only get madder and attack with more ferocity.

Before you even think of stepping outside the safety of the training hall to use your devastating fighting style to beat someone into submission, I'd like you to consider the following statement that I once heard: "Son, you hit me and I find out about it . . . you'll be in a heap o' trouble."

The older man who said that was not afraid of pain. He was also about six feet four and weighed nearly 300 pounds. If the would-be tough guy's blow created only pain and not other effects to prevent a counterattack, my friend would have crushed the punk. The man was like a juggernaut. You could not stand in front of him and try to stop him by inflicting pain. He'd just steamroll over you before you could hurt him enough to stop him. In fact, the more you hurt him, the harder he'd crush you.

Pain and emotion are motivational messages. When we feel them, we feel we must act. That is a critical component of effective control tactics/submission restraints. If you don't want your opponent to react, don't send that message.

This motivational aspect is also important to understand when you try to nickel-and-dime someone to death with the problems you are creating for him. If all you do is hurt him rather than check his ability to attack you, he will counterattack even more ferociously.

Yes, you may have smacked him and caused him pain; B.F.D. That is far less important then the fact that your blow moved him farther out of position to counterattack, off-balanced him slightly, weakened his structure for a second, and overloaded his neural network (shocked his system). This made it harder for him to come up with counters to the rapidly stacking problems you caused. These are the IBRs that you create and exploit. You don't just hurt him and hope that pain will make the big bad man stop attacking and go away.

Have you ever heard that you must soften someone up before applying a joint lock or throw? Consider that advice in the context of what I have just said. I'm not there to soften him up; I'm there to trash his structure. What's more, realize the importance of not letting your opponent regain his structure after you have disrupted it. You don't open the window and then let him close it again. You must exploit the reaction that you create before he can undo your efforts.

That is what softening him up means: weakening his structure before you attempt the next move, not beating him into submission. And a weakened structure is one that you can more easily manipulate because he can't resist you and gravity at the same time.

Pain, if it does anything, just interferes with his ability to find an effective answer to these problems in time. It takes his mind off coming up with a good response to what is happening. It's just one more roadblock to getting back to what he wants.

With this in mind, let me give you three standards EVERY move you make should meet.

1. It needs to secure your perimeter (protecting you from a counteroffense)
2. It needs to disrupt his structure/disturb his orientation (removing his ability to effectively counterattack)
3. It needs to set up your next offensive (your next move is right there with no prep time)

Ensuring that every move you do meets these criteria is not something that you can do without intense critical analysis and understanding of fundamentals. But when you can meet these criteria, your offense will begin to resemble a pool shark running the table. It will never be the other guy's turn.

I said it once, I'll say it again: Contending with an effective offense is indeed like fighting a swarm of stinging bees. There is just too much going wrong at once. And what's more, it is never the same kind of problem that is popping up, one after the other.

I have an acronym that I use to describe different types of offense. It's not a good one; in fact, it's rather stupid. It's Dr. Pitt & Co. (Think of Groucho Marx meeting the Three Stooges.) It stands for

DRive
Pull
Impact
Twist
Takedown &
COmpression

Dr. Pitt & Co is like primary colors. These colors (constituting hue) and black and white (value) are the source of all the colors you see. It's just a matter of the proportions they are mixed in to create a particular color. Dr. Pitt & Co is a summation of all the primary attack modes. Granted, these are variations of push/ pull, but when you understand them and their effects you can tailor your actions to meet these very effective building codes.

Any type of attack, from any style, is either a single example of one of these or of a combination of them. A boxing jab is obviously an impact. An *osoto gari* combines several of these in the series of moves that make up that technique, and it all comes under the category of a takedown. In order for that technique to work, however, all those elements must be present.

Compression is basically taking something and squishing it between a force and a base. Checking a hockey player into the boards is a prime example of a compression attack. Compression attacks are so effective because they do not allow the person being attacked to move away from the force. The force is not any greater, but the attack hurts more because the force cannot be bled off by moving with it.

Almost anything can be used as a base. The main trick is to come in on the correct angle in order to drive him into it. A simple, straight, horizontal punch becomes far more powerful when you have placed your other hand behind your target.

Things get even worse if your back hand accelerates him into your first. When this happens, you literally push him into your punch, or—if it has turned into an unlimited/total-offense situation—into your elbow. In this maneuver both your hands are moving along the same line, toward a head-on collision.

You can get this idea by simply punching into your open palm. You literally clap with a fist and palm. But don't just do this perpendicular to your chest, move your hands around; punch out,

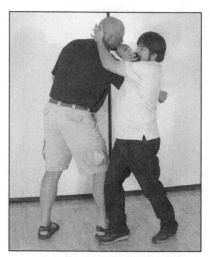

Prep with hand behind and fist in front.

Compression hit.

up, and down. Look at the angles along which your blows are moving and see how your other hand has to come in on that same angle, but from another direction. Then try this on the heavy bag. As you hit with a fist in one direction, slap with the open hand from the opposite direction. You will find that you generally have to limit this to short-range punches, elbows, and knees. You will also notice that the bag doesn't swing, but jumps, when hit. That indicates that the power is going where you want it to go.

Another way to create a compression attack is by coming in on the diagonal. My favorite is to use the earth as a base. Your blow comes down into your opponent, trapping him between your force and the earth.

It is not straight down; it is a downward diagonal. If you came straight down, your attempts to compress him would compete with his structure's ability to resist gravity. In order to effectively break his structure this way, you have to hit super hard. Unless you are physically massive, it would be difficult to generate enough force. This is not to say that such a blow wouldn't hurt. It would

Prep for diagonal hit.　　　　　　　　*Hit.*

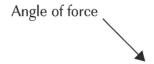

Angle of force

hurt like hell. The problem is that his skeletal structure would most likely bounce back into place before you had time to exploit his IBR. This is especially true because to generate enough force to break his structure with a straight downward strike, you would have to move to an extreme position, out far enough that it would be difficult for you to continue to press your attack. You'd have to come back to a better position, thereby adding extra moves.

Coming in on the diagonal creates several advantages. First, it is far enough off-angle that his structure cannot effectively resist. Second, although close to down, there is enough lateral force to allow the effects of your strike to be enhanced by gravity. Third, it doesn't push him back nearly as much as it pushes him down. Instead of sending him reeling away from you, you keep him in range for your next offensive. Until he reestablishes his structure, he cannot effectively counterattack.

Line of
incoming
force

Original
VA

Diagonal hit.

*Angle of force/structural
collapse.*

Fourth, by breaking his structure in this downward manner you put him in the grip of gravity. That isn't a "can be ignored" issue. Gravity is a *"must be addressed"* issue, especially when it has a hold on him. Furthermore, there is a very good chance that he will not be able to get a foot out to reestablish his structure. The ensuing fall is less about his losing his balance (although that is part of it) than lack of support. Getting a foot out in time when you have lost your balance is easy compared to getting sufficient structure under a falling body, especially one that isn't falling straight down, but diagonally.

Fifth, even if he does manage to get a foot out fast enough to keep from hitting the deck, he will not be in balance. For a split second he will be teetering. He won't have regained full structure or balance yet. And when someone is wobbling like this, it is the easiest and best time to move him where you want him. He has neither his weight on the ground nor the structure to resist your moving him.

This teetering is the IBR you want. If you have delivered this blow with the Big 3, he will be faced with two basic choices in order to stay upright: buckle his structure and try to reestablish it (riskier), or pivot (safer). Most people take the first choice because they are not familiar with being hit on this angle or with having a blow create a compressing effect. Too bad they picked the least effective response.

While teetering is the preferred IBR, the very least you can rely on is his knees buckling. As he is trying to straighten back up, grab him and either uproot him or drag him down.

If your opponent pivots and sheds the force, it tells you that you have treed yourself a bad one. The counter to this kind of diagonal attack is to start to go down with the force but move your vertical axis off the line of the force (weight transfer), then allow it to push your body into a pivot. This is not a response that people tend to find on their own. If you feel this counter coming, my first advice is to jump back. This kind of counter makes it extremely easy for the opponent to turn this pivot into a counterattack and your kidneys into guacamole. Yes, there are things you can do to counter his counter—and their roots are found in this book. The details, however, are beyond the scope of this text.

Get two friends who are familiar with the concepts in this book and obtain some chest protection. Two of the people should practice these kinds of blows while the third observes and comments. When hitting, aim for the protected chest and watch for the IBR. If the person being struck goes reeling too far back, the hit was too horizontal. If the person buckles and springs right back up, the blow was too vertical. If the person has real trouble keeping from falling, the angle is correct. If you don't have time to exploit the IBR you created, you are in the wrong position.

After you each get the hang of doing these kinds of attack, begin to practice the counter. It is important to have the counter ingrained before moving on to the next step, which is to have the person wearing the chest protector attack and the other person parry/counter/deflect while starting to move into fence. As the person arrives in fence, deliver this blow to the hogue-wearer's chest. Now the game's afoot. Is he fast enough to counter, or have you set up fence well enough not only to keep him from shedding, but to exploit the reaction you create with another hit, twist, or pull?

This exercise amounts to one-step sparring, with an attitude. Either of you is allowed one offense after the compression attack; then you have to break. The question is, who is going to get that last offense? Again, do this with three people, so everyone gets a chance to both participate and watch. You will learn as much by watching this game as you will by playing it.

In addition—and to save your hands—you will find that slaps tend to work faster and better than hammer fists in creating these kinds of compression attack. Combining different angles will give you interesting results. One slap breaks his structure, the next compresses in a different direction or knocks him totally off balance. This is how I can drop someone with just two fast slaps.

There are thousands of ways to attack with compression. In fact, if you look at it closely you will see that a huge portion of submission fighting and grappling is made up of these kinds of attack. Put opponents where they can't escape, and then squeeze. You will also discover that this idea plays a very important part in both armbar and control tactics and throws (in which you drag him over your base in order to throw him).

Before leaving this subject, I wish to introduce you to one of the most effective manifestations of this kind of attack. It is what my friend Bob Orlando calls *scissoring*.

Earlier on page 173, I explained the idea of how two hits can be on a head-on collision course by following the same line. Scissoring denotes opposing forces on parallel lines. The two forces don't collide, but pass each other like cars heading in opposite directions on the same street.

Parallel lines of force

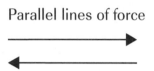

If you think about it in terms of cars passing, you can get an idea of how destructive this move can be. Imagine one of those cars, hitting a creature that gets in its way. Now imagine what would happen to that poor creature if it were hit simultaneously by both cars—each hitting the creature but narrowly missing one another. What action would that creature, now a carcass, undergo?

It would spin and flip.

You can create that same reaction in your opponent by stepping in and hitting on opposing parallel lines, one high and one low. With a practice partner—*and very gently*—try punching low to the abdominal area while slapping the head in the opposite direction. Depending on where you strike, you will get radically different results . . . although they are all spectacular. You can practice this hard on the heavy bag, but please do not go full speed on your training partners.

I want you to pay very close attention to the application of this idea in kicks. A kick that delivers force at a distance takes on entirely new dimensions when done up close and with a counterforce. By this I mean grabbing your opponent and pulling him into a kick/knee delivered at close range. This is something else that you need to practice full force on a bag and gently with your partner. It doesn't take much force to destroy someone's structure in this manner.

I have already mentioned the difference between a drive and an impact: an impact is aimed at the vertical axis whereas a drive goes beyond it.

The purpose of a drive is to move things. Whether to push things away from you or toward you, it moves your opponent to right where you want him—not only in range for your next attack, but also into the best position to take the full force.

Why bother reaching when it's easier to knock him into where it is going to hurt the most?

Here is an example. I always had problems with Figure 4 locks. It was too difficult for me to move into position fast enough to catch a punch. It was Steve Plinck who pointed out that I was wasting my time trying; it was easier and faster to parry/strike his punching limb into hyperextension, using the outside of an inward-circling action. This knocks his punch into my waiting other hand. That parry/strike from behind not only hyperextends his limb and puts it into range for the Figure 4, but also breaks his structure and stalls or interferes with his retraction as he teeters while trying to regain his balance and structure. This buys me extra time to drop the Figure 4 on him.

It never ceases to amaze me how people try to drive when they should be impacting, and vice versa. Even a simple hook-uppercut combination has a different effect if you focus on making the hook more of a drive than a hit. Your hook pushes him into the freight train that is your uppercut. All it takes is going beyond the vertical axis and leaving your hook out there as an obstacle to keep him from regaining his structure or moving him where you want him to step.

Ready, incoming punch.

Parry/drive from behind.

Into trap.

Breaking his structure.

Figure 4 lock.

One of my favorite ways to use a drive is actually by creating a giant twist. You not only intentionally go beyond his vertical axis, but do it as far away from his VA as possible. This creates a giant wheel, with his VA as the hub. You spin him around his

Ready.

Extending limb to shoulder. Ready to pull.

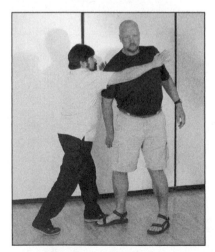

Stepping in and spinning the wheel with pull and drive.

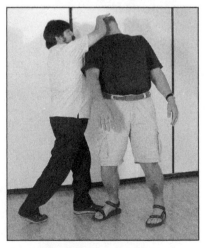

Another kind of drive into a take down.

hub. This not only destroys his orientation (hence his ability to attack), but puts him into a teetering position and makes him extremely vulnerable to an impact. (When something is twisted, it creates its own base against itself, and as such cannot shed or move away from incoming force.)

Notice that there are two separate drives here: one with the right hand and a second with the left. What starts as a pull with the left turns into a drive. The source of power for both is your moving into fence. This is the easiest way to create a twist with drive/impact combo. There are better ways that are harder to resist, but start practicing with this one, since it is closer to familiar impact attacks.

Twisting or driving your opponent off his line of forward orientation is critical for surviving unlimited- or total-offense situations. If you don't break his orientation so that he has to stop and reset in order to continue attacking, there is a good chance that his attack will succeed.

This doesn't sound too bad until you realize that I am talking about his having a weapon in his hand. The limited-offense situation has turned out to be an unlimited one. That is not the kind of situation in which you want to stand and trade attacks in order to see who folds first. This is why fence, destroying his orientation and keeping him from moving back into attack position, is so critical.

Having said that, however, let me point out that taking someone off orientation by driving is also an instrumental part of effective strategy for limited-offense situations—especially if you are trying to control someone. Spinning him and twisting his structure makes getting him into a control hold ten times easier.

You might want to practice having your partner attack you and, as he does, spinning him as you move into fence and then

Flailing.

Spin the wheel.

*Break balance/low blow
(sentry removal).*

*On the ground wrapped up (full nelson
with leg wraps).*

dropping him into your favorite submission hold. You will find
that some holds work better than others. If your favorite doesn't
work from that position, experiment to see what does.

Notice that in this series, after "spinning the wheel" there
is a low line drive with the unseen left hand to further break his

structure while the upper limb creates a scissoring effect. Your weight drags him down and you wrap him up.

I would not recommend this series unless you have a backup partner who can assist in extracting you. While this move minimizes the damage to both you and the person you are controlling (i.e., no chokehold is applied), it does not leave you in a strategic position. You will find that to handle another opponent this move is useful if your backup is inexperienced or is too far away (unfortunately, the two are often synonymous) when it is necessary to do the takedown.

Another advantage is that even if your training partner doesn't attack, but instead either flails wildly or stands there in passive defiance (the "go ahead, arrest me" stance), you will blast him into the position to be controlled. Often, if you hit hard enough with your first drive, his arm will helicopter right up into your waiting hand (of course, it helps to drop your hand into position to catch it). *Spin the wheel* is one of my favorite ways to put someone into an armbar. It's fast, easy, and easily defended in court. You spin him, catch his arm, and just step right into an armbar.

Let's talk again about goofing around. If your training partner starts to resist, you can begin to soften him up with various love taps. Experiment with different moves and find the ones that you do best, then focus on perfecting them. The IBR you create should destroy his ability to resist being spun.

Armbars are splendid examples of a combination of compression and drive attacks. The base is not higher up. It is your grabbing (pulling) hand, farther down the limb. The leverage is created by driving his shoulder past that base, not by bringing his limb past a higher base. There are two reasons for this. First, if you make the hand lower down his arm do the work, there is a good chance you will lever him out of position. You will catapult him away from you and out of fence position.

"Go ahead, arrest me" stance.

Spin the wheel.

Turn right hand over to catch
helicopter/left hand pushes.

Pull/drive/step into arm bar.

The second is that by using the hand closest to his shoulder as the drive, you far more effectively destroy his structure. Make it a downward diagonal drive and his structure and balance will

Driving arm far up shoulder palm down (okay).

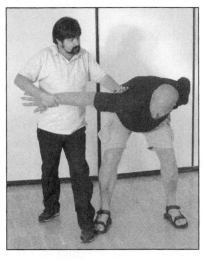

Driving arm between shoulder and elbow palm down (better).

Driving arm in shoulder joint, palm up (best).

begin to crumble. From there all you have to do is pivot and kneel. He will be eating dirt.

Although it will work against other parts of the body, it is best to apply the drive into the shoulder joint.

I prefer to use the back of my arm instead of either my hand or the palm side of my forearm. I like this for several reasons. One, by looking at my palm I am less likely to "chicken wing" and leave my lower ribs and abdomen exposed by accidentally raising my elbow. Two, although the difference is a fraction of a second, I can drop my elbow faster to protect my ribs from this position. Three, with my palm facing me I am in a much stronger structural position to resist force in close (e.g. if his counter is an attempted clinch). Four, because of the angle and the decreased chance of chicken winging, there is far less chance of my arm's slipping off him as he struggles. Five, I can apply more pressure through structure, not through muscle, but by dropping my weight.

With my palm facing away from me, however, the force I can apply is mostly based on muscle. You can see this in a quick experiment with your partner. Have him stand with his hand out, palm up. His job is to resist. Place your palm down on his and try to push his hand down. Flip your hand over and, keeping your elbow close to your side, begin to push down. If you run into too much resistance, just bend your knees as you push.

On top of everything else, with the palm-down position there is a greater chance of your chicken winging if he resists.

Drives against joints and any other part of the body that "folds" are particularly effective. In fact, strikes against the inside of the joints represent one of the few instances in which I agree with the idea that blocks are hits. But in those cases, it really is less a block and more a drive that causes the arm to fold. In this case, the drive keeps on going. Just make sure that your other hand is in position to trap or catch what you create.

There are countless other ways to use drives in order to move your opponent into position where you can do nasty things to his body. Whatever system you use, pay attention to the difference between *touching the vertical axis* and *hacking through it*. In fact,

Incoming blow (defender thumb to nose) (attacker w/heavy blow).

Moving/hitting inside of elbow.

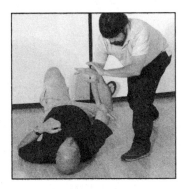

Driving him over.

Wrapping him up.

some of the most devastating kicks from muay Thai aren't de-signed to go into the leg, but to cut it down like a tree. Now imagine what would happen if you had pushed or pulled him so that he was teetering over that leg . . .

— 12 —

Different Offenses: Pulling

In maneuver warfare, we attempt not to destroy the entire enemy force, but to render most of it irrelevant.

—Lt. Col. Robert Leonhard, U.S. Army

Pulling your opponent is one of the most underrated and least frequently applied tactics among Western fighters. There are many significant differences in body movement and action among Eastern and Western fighting styles. Pulling is one of them. I say this about Western fighters' vulnerability because even when they use Oriental fighting styles, Westerners tend to use too much pushing. This overemphasis on pushing leaves most Western fighters vulnerable to pulling attacks—especially those that take them off an angle.

Conversely, however, I also have seen practitioners of those Eastern arts that rely on using an attacker's force against him thoroughly savaged when facing someone who knew how to deliver power through correct body movement, structure, and, most important, range. You don't mess with a boxer. Unfortunately for the person in the gentle arts, a lack of overcommitment by an opponent who can still deliver force spells serious trouble. The fast and dangerous feet of a boxer allow him to move in and out of range as effectively as any Oriental-style practitioner. He counters the other's counters while not exposing his structure or balance through movement and blows.[1]

When people ask me about strike enhancers, my response is to snort, "Learn to hit!" A closed fist around an item removes your ability to grab, slap, gouge, and all the many other options that make the open hand of someone who knows what he is doing such a dangerous weapon. There is, however, another important benefit. Someone who knows how to use the Big 3 is going to be far less vulnerable to pulling attacks than someone who doesn't.

Remember how I said that trying to hit someone in the wrong range will destroy your structure? Bad structure and leaning to reach destroy your balance. That is exactly what pulling attacks exploit! You're halfway there, and a pull will take you the rest of the way.

The ability to use range, body movement, and structure will do wonders to keep pulling attacks from working on you. That is because you aren't overextended. It will also go miles in helping you to grasp how you can use the Big 3 against people who, because they don't understand range, are sacrificed to the rules of structure and range. That makes them really vulnerable to pulls.

There are two essential components to pull attacks. In fact, these can be considered fundamentals. They are (1) take up the slack, and (2) move your body downward.

There's an old mechanic's saw: "If a car ain't starting, you ain't getting either fuel or fire." If you follow these two fundamentals

---

1. This is exactly why I am such an advocate of cross-training in different systems besides your main one, and grappling. There are much more out there than those two. Cross-training shows you the myriad types of attack that are available, and why you should respect them.

until you find where either the fuel or the fire has stopped, you will find your problem.

In the same vein not taking up enough slack or insufficient downward motion can almost always be found at the roots of why a pulling attack falls. These two standards are building codes that must be met.

Let's look at the most basic pulling attack. It is also an effective maneuver against passive resisters, i.e., opponents who refuse to move.

The grab is made as close to the wrist as possible to allow a better grip. Grabbing at the wrist keeps you from sliding down his arm. The swell of the wrist gives you a handle. You can put your hands higher up on his forearm, slide down, and then grip at the wrist, but don't try to grab while your hand is too high up.

In stepping back and down, you start "eating up" the slack of his arm. The first part of your weight transfer destroys his structure. Near the end of the transfer you accelerate him with a sharp downward pull of the arm. Don't try to speed up his fall until you have broken his structure. Your muscles aren't the source of the power; the weight transfer is. Your muscles accelerate his fall and keep him from recovering.

This is one of the most basic pulls because it teaches you to focus on the two fundamentals. Your initial movement eats up the slack in his arm. Once you have done this, you have created a direct line to his vertical axis that carries force directly to it. As your motion continues back and down, the results start to manifest. Often, he will spin on his VA before being pulled forward. This tends to twist him off line and can often prevent him from even getting a foot out in time to save himself. If he does manage to get his foot out, there is little chance that he will be able to keep from being pulled into a teetering position by your

Grab.

Eat slack, sneak other hand up his arm.

Weight transfer, weight over rear leg/torso upright (break his structure).

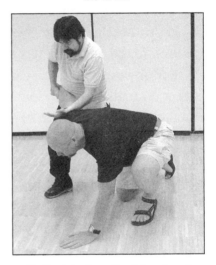

Pull with pivot (lead hand used to accelerate him/drive).

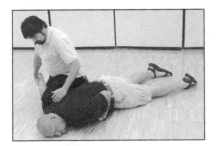

Becomes a drive with just a little more pivot, stepping, and kneeling.

diagonally backward weight transfer. Once he begins to fall, you accelerate him to prevent his getting a foot out in time. If you do not meet the criteria of "eat slack, move body down," there is a good chance that this move will not work. Although the puller leans forward initially to lengthen the step, he drops his center with the weight transfer to the rear leg.

While this pull/throw is extremely basic, it requires that you practice weight transfer and coherent body movement to the point where you can do them smoothly, quickly, and easily. It also requires you to be aware of what it feels like when someone's structure is intact and, conversely, when it is broken. Trying to accelerate him before you have broken his balance tends to make the move less effective . . . if it works at all.

For obvious safety reasons, don't practice this kind of throw except on mats and with someone with tumbling experience—if not under the supervision of a judo or aikido sensei or tumbling coach. In fact, it is recommended that you do all your training under professional supervision. A trained individual who is acquainted with the concepts in this book will be able to spot problems faster and is likely to be more aware of safety concerns.

Having said that, let me also give you a bit of practice advice: let go early enough so that your training partner has time to tuck and roll. Remember this is for training purposes. What you want to ingrain in both your conscious mind and your puppy brain is eating up the slack and breaking his structure through correct body movement and range. Once you have done this he will start to fall. In a live-fire situation you want to hang on and quickly drop. If you do so, he will not have time to reestablish his base and structure and he will go down, hard. By slowing the descent over a less steep incline (angle), he will not hit as hard. Once you have created a connection to his VA and broken his balance/structure, how hard he lands is entirely up to you. The degree of downward angle, the time you let go, and your descent speed will greatly increase the impact a person sustains. As such, learn to control how fast and how hard you drop someone. This skill can and will save you all kinds of trouble in court.

Although they can be extremely vicious and excruciating, pulling attacks are generally best deployed to destroy structure and balance, shift orientation, create a teetering effect, and move an opponent into the crosshairs of something really nasty. This is not exactly a setup move in which you are wasting time, getting ready to attack. You are attacking through indirect means. Remember how I said that pain is not necessarily an objective of an attack? This is an example of that kind of wider thinking. If your definition of an attack has to include pain, you won't see the goal. In lieu of causing pain, this tactic attacks his ability to attack you.

One of the fastest and most effective spots to grab for a pull is inside the elbow. The humerus connects the elbow to the shoulder. The shoulder performs a wide degree of circular motion because of its pivot design. That pivot, however, is not designed to stretch. It does create a direct line to the VA when moved in or away. That means you use his upper arm to either push him over or pull him down.

Our skeletal structure is capable of resisting force better in some positions than others. We have an ability to resist force coming from in front of us. Force can be applied to your opponent from many directions other than straight in, however. These represent ways that he will not be able to resist as well. Forces along these lines can often shock his structure and buy you extra time to move into position.

An elbow held out from the body at a 45-degree angle is a tempting target for someone who knows that the humerus can be used as a conduit for force into the VA. A sharp, fast blow on that same angle transfers force into him. You know the effect if you have ever had someone put his elbow against your side, make a fist with that same hand, and then sharply rap his knuckles. Hitting the fist in the same direction in which the arm runs transfers the force of the blow into your ribs. The jolting effect of a fast, sharp strike up his humerus is a useful trick if you are unexpectedly confronted with an elbow while trying to move into fence.

Pulling along the line created by his upper arm is a sneaky trick that most Western fighters don't expect. The same direct line to his VA is there, and he is less able to resist a pull than a push.

The fastest formula to use is this: *Pull his elbow to the floor; tug it down the line in which it is pointing.*

Even if he bends his arm, his elbow points toward that same spot. You pull him along this line. The odds are, this simple example will not work against a sober person. It can, but you would have to time the pull when his foot is lifted, as in a step or attempted kick. This requires awfully good timing. If you have a sober person teetering in this manner, you will have to switch to another technique—a Figure 4 lock or an armbar spring immediately to mind, as either move will finish the destruction of his structure. Less reliable, but faster, would be adding a drive/impact into his opposite shoulder on the same line you are pulling him down.

On the other hand, this simple pulling takedown tends to work very well against drunks. This is especially true if you first pull away from him horizontally, near his shoulder level. This short horizontal pull drags him into a teetering position and sets him up for the downward diagonal drag. It doesn't have to be much, just enough to weight his leg and eat up the slack.

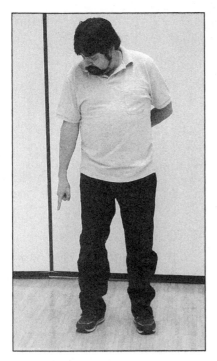

Pointing in direction of pull.

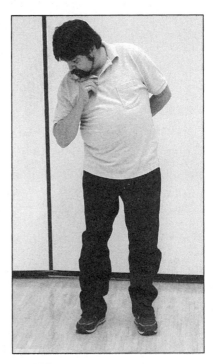

Elbow pointing to same spot.

Pulling down.

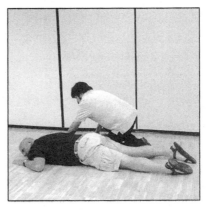

Take down.

I have used this tactic many times against quarrelsome drunks, and a few sober people, as well. All it takes is a fast grab and pull of his elbow. OK, so you might want to spice it up with a step to the side, pulling him horizontally before pulling down.[2]

A particularly useful variation can be used against a wildly flailing person whom you must control. The problem with a person's flailing his arms is that you cannot predict where his limb will be. But once you've caught an arm, it's easy.

This technique also works if you are not exactly in a good position. It can make up for all kinds of distance problems. Preparation for this move requires that you put your rear hand up near your face. (In fact, I often teach this as "thumbing your nose at an opponent." When training officers, however, we call it the "fighter's salute," so they don't get in trouble with the brass.) Bending your other arm just a little lets you "wipe up" the same angle that you did with the shoulder slap. The entire arm is used in a large sweep that, like a parry, goes deep into his territory and returns toward your shoulder.

When you have your hands in position, step in on a slight outside angle as you windmill up the angle. This doesn't have to be a big step. In fact, you step only into range of his elbow. If he is lunging toward you, you don't have to step at all; he's coming to you. With this sweep you hook his elbow with yours. When you first practice this, it's advisable to wait until his arm has crossed the centerline and is moving toward the same side as your wiping arm. In time you can experiment with catching it anywhere, no matter what direction it is going in, but you won't be able to do that at first.

---

2. A nice combination move—especially against a larger opponent—is to use a horizontal drive against the side of his head with one hand while pulling his elbow with the other. Once you have his weight moving, you "kneel and pray."

Fighter's salute and crooked windmill upper diagonal sweep.

After knocking, running through fire.

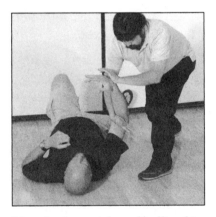

Transferring weight and pulling him off balance while starting Figure 4.

Turn and kneel with opponent in Figure 4.

A small, but important point: Don't turn your hips as you enter/step. Try to go in as straight as possible. Once you hook him, you can start turning your hips. If you use your hip turn to catch, you have less runway in which to get the job done. You want all the energy of the hip turn to go into him and for the full distance; you do not want to waste half of it in eating up slack.

When your arm connects, bend it even more and create a hook to gaff and drag him where you want him to go. Your swinging arm should intercept his arm and start bringing it toward the opposite side of your face . . . and right into your waiting opposite hand. If you are good, you can just turn this into a Figure 4 as you transfer your weight backward from that position.

If, however, you are not the reincarnation of Bruce Lee, you might want to get him into a Figure 4 using a more basic method. I call this position "running through fire." It is what I showed in the illustration on the previous page. Instead of doing it with your hands, you move him into position with your forearms. The position you end up taking is as though you are running through flames.

You do this as you shift your weight backward and pull him off balance. Often, you won't be able to grab his arm with your hand, but you will be able to trap his forearm against yours. Drag his arm into your waiting limb (notice I didn't say "hand"?). Expect a crash, so make sure that you have structure. It's OK if his limb isn't perfectly in your hand because all you do, while keeping his limb pinned against your forearm, is raise your elbows as though you are trying to protect your face while running through a fire. However, and this is important, don't just lift your elbow. Even though you are pulling him backward with one limb, you push into his arm with your guard arm. When you lift your elbow, you also scoop up his, as well as get your elbow out of the way of your windmill limb. This brings his wrist into a position where you can more easily catch it (especially if it runs into your other arm). It also further twists his structure. In addition, it brings your other hand close to the inside of his elbow. That hand/forearm serves as a source of impact to start his arm folding and as a fulcrum for your leverage.

From the running-through-fire position, slightly change the angle of your movements and start a "twiddling forearms" motion that rolls up his arm in a *Figure 4 lock*. An important point to remember is that the twiddling forearms don't go straight into your chest, but instead veer off on an angle. This is easier to think of if you just do the Figure 4 *in the direction in which you will be heading*. You're going to be turning and kneeling anyway, so just start rolling up the "hose" (his arm) in the direction in which you will be turning. The combination of the Figure 4 and the kneeling pivot should keep him from running into you—or effectively attacking as he is being taken down.

Even though you have your guard hand in the fighter's salute to protect you, expect to get clipped when you close against a flailing person. The blow won't be hard, because (a) you will have your guard up to take its brunt and (b) flailing strikes very seldom have the Big 3 behind them, since they are not intentional blows. They are closer to what most people think of as slaps. The reason you are likely to get clipped is that if you have your hand on center line you are in a better position to fold his limb when you move in on an angle. You pay for this long-term advantage by leaving part of your face exposed. I should warn you, however, that if you protect your face by moving off center line, you run the risk of being in a worse position to roll up his arm. So you pay for the short term in the long term. With a little practice, however, you can avoid these problems. Instead of passively saluting him, simply parry his elbow into your wiping arm.[3]

---

3. Another way to improve this is, when you are able to parry effectively, do a double-parry in a scissoring action. Instead of hooking elbows, parry inside his elbow while your other parry causes his arm to fold. Using your fingers instead of a hooked elbow as the fulcrum point allows you greater control over the force of the takedown. With little or no practice you will find that elbow to elbow is good; with some practice you will find that the fingertips work much better.

This kind of takedown-and-control move is useful when you have to immediately control someone without causing too much damage. While takedown and controls are usually done better and easier with two against one, sometimes you just can't wait for backup to arrive or the CERT team to suit up. You will have to do the job yourself as you run up to the problem. It is a good technique for stopping a one-sided assault. I have also used this tactic to break up fights, but more as a throw instead of turning my back to the other combatant. In this case you can use it as a nondamaging stalling move that gives your backup time to arrive. Don't try to use it to end a serious fight single-handedly, as the controlling part ties up your hands and prevents you from defending yourself. If you can pick and choose, use it on the most aggressive member of a conflict. It is extremely disorienting and, with the Figure 4 in place if you crank it, very painful. The combination of being spun like a top and threatened with extreme pain as the cost of further bad behavior tends to take even the most aggressive person out of fighting mode (psychotics notwithstanding, but you will have them on the floor and in a Figure 4).

As a final point, this is not a muscle move. It relies more on leverage, weight transfer, and destruction of his structure. Once you have caught his arm and started the weight transfer, there is no need for muscle. The manipulation of his VA through his limbs will easily drop him. This is a situation in which you must have faith in the laws of physics and in what will happen if you get him into this position. If you meet code on this move, there is no need for muscle; you will pull him over.

If you remember to pull his elbow toward the ground, you can use pulling attacks with great effect, not only to clear the patch and rattle his structure, but to move into position. One of the sneakiest ways I know to use this attack is to pull yourself into fence. You do this much the same way you would pull yourself along a secured rope.

You don't try to grab your opponent in a typical finger-and-thumb grip. That is too slow, and creates all kinds of problems with grabbing an incoming attack—not the least of which is a good chance of breaking or straining your thumb. What I teach students to do is called *gaffing*. Fold your hand into a thumb-out hitchhiking position. Notice that your fingertips curl into your palm. This grab is done with that fingertip curl. It creates a structure that can deliver a small but very effective compression attack.

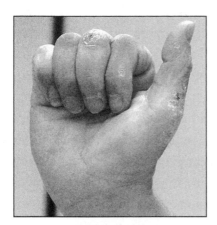

Hitchhiker (gaff).

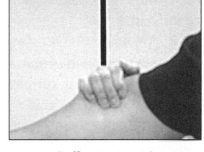

Gaffing into muscle.

Gaffing into skin.

Gaffing into clothing.

The nice thing about gaffing is that what it catches in its grip doesn't matter. It will grip everything with equal ease as your fingertips drive into your palm. And it is self-adjusting: if your fingers can't get into the muscle and hook him, they will slide until they catch skin and pinch. If they can't catch skin, they'll take cloth. Whatever is caught is caught, and its connection to the VA is exploited.

Gaffing can be done as fast as it takes for you to curl your fingers, which makes it work very well in combination with parries and openhanded strikes. Literally, if you can put a hand on someone, you can gaff him and then pull. As Rick Hernandez says, "A grab is just a hit that hangs on." Once you begin to think this way, you will see that with some practice, a blow that rocks someone also creates a whiplash effect that will bring him right into your waiting hand. It's just a matter of not retracting all the way.

Anytime you can get your hand on the inside of someone's elbow, you are in position for a pulling attack. Because the shoulder's pivot doesn't stretch, humans are susceptible to quick downward jerks from this position. If you push down, it is a drive. While that works, if the person is larger and stronger, he can resist somewhat. But if you dip your center (bend your knees) as you jerk, your body weight pulls him down, with less size-related resistance.

Although I have stated that inflicting pain is far less important than destroying structure and off-balancing an opponent, at times you need moves that cause extreme pain. Usually, these involve a combination of compression, twisting, and pulling.

Sound unlikely?

Image someone gaffing your crotch and then "looking at his watch."

Pulling away from the body destroys structure. While such moves can be painful, they tend not to be when you move this way. Pulling attacks that hurt work not by pulling away from the body, but by moving along it. For example, grabbing someone's earlobe and pulling it away from his head won't have much effect. It will hurt him and rock his head, but you will usually lose your grip before any damage is done. The same grip while twisting/pulling/lifting along his head will have far more effect. It will also tend to reorient his head as he tries to move away from the pain. Since this is an extreme measure, I don't recommend that you play around with it. If you are going to try it, do it gently and under professional supervision.

I would like you to see where the pulling aspects can be found in any takedown or throwing technique. I assure you that you will notice a great deal of pulling, which will come in many flavors. In fact, run your favorite techniques through Dr. Pitt & Co to see how these aspects are present in what you already do. You will find countless examples of what I have been talking about in recent chapters.

~ 13 ~

Different Offenses: Twisting and Takedowns

*The more usual reason for adopting a strategy of limited aim
is that of change in the balance of force. . . .*

*The essential condition of such a strategy is that the drain on
him should be disproportionately greater than on oneself.*

—Sir Basil Liddel-Hart

One of the fundamental differences between a pull and a twist
is that in order for a pull to work, the slack must be taken out,
whereas twist automatically takes out that slack. From there it
is just a matter of what you do with it. Any action on your part
after that—other than letting him go—*will be effective.*

Although limb folds and joint locks make up a large part
of twisting attacks, there exists another type of move, a twist,
which is not allowed in the sports ring or any civilized dojo.
This is because twists exponentially increase the likelihood of
damage. They can—and will—seriously hurt people.

The way to approach twists is to understand that they work
best when followed by something else. The question of what
comes next depends on the situation. A twist followed by a

ferocious impact is designed to shatter things. A twist followed by either a pull or drive that you loosen up in time (to allow the person to "unwind" before he hits the ground) is good as a control tactic. When a twist is followed by the same but you don't let go, you have to get a lawyer to help explain to the authorities why it was necessary to hurt him so badly. If you don't allow him to unwind before slamming him into the ground, you are going to cause serious damage.

When applied forcibly and without checks or restraint, twists will cause damage. If the damage wasn't justified, you are going to be in some serious trouble. So approach the subject of twisting with both caution and a firm understanding of use-of-force laws. Knowing that *a little can go a long way*, don't overdo it.

Nowhere else are the issues of structure, balance, and orientation so amazingly manifest as in twisting attacks. Once you are familiar with these principles, seeing how a twist attack exploits them should make you feel as if you have just gotten a free pass to a gourmet buffet. The delightful possibilities are amazing. You literally are limited only by your imagination. These kinds of attack not only work by themselves, but exponentially increase the effectiveness of everything else you do. What would otherwise take six moves now can be done in two.

Having said that, however, now that you have this power, the onus of learning how to use it responsibly is on you.

Twists are like power tools. While it is true that they get the job done faster, accidents happen faster, too. As with power tools, a thorough understanding of safety procedures must be in place before you attempt to apply twists. Twists are not something that you put into the "if I ever had to use this stuff," macho huffing-and-puffing list. They belong in the *"when you use them, these are the realities that must be addressed"* category.

The fastest takedown I know involves simply rolling the person's head onto his shoulders and walking past him. Peyton Quinn coined the term The Alien for his version, in which you put your hand on his face and roll his head so that his face points toward the ceiling. Without losing structure and using slight downward push, you just walk forward. If you have seen any of the *Alien* movies, the hand on the face looks just like the alien "face hugger."

Here you will see a prime example of what I meant by knowing that it will work (faith) and having the responsibility to learn how much force to apply. This move, when applied with enough force and when the person is not allowed to unwind (i.e., twist or do some other move to soften the impact), can be fatal. If you kneel down and accelerate his fall with arm muscle without releasing him, there is a very good chance that he could suffer a fatal injury. Cracking his head open on the concrete had better be in response to his offering you an "immediate threat of death or grave bodily injury." Otherwise you will be facing a manslaughter charge.

Unfortunately, the same thing can happen if the guy is too drunk and doesn't twist in time—even if released early enough in the move. This is why if I want to control the person without hurting him, I prefer to move his chin over his shoulder before doing this move. Once his chin is on his shoulder, you then roll his head as though you were trying to put his ear onto his shoulder blade, thereby creating a saving twist in motion as he falls.[1]

The Alien is a stripped-down version of a far more complicated Aikido technique. Manipulation of the head in order to destroy structure is not the sole property of Aikido. In fact, it is very common in Chinese, Indonesian, and Malaysian systems.

Extending someone's limb while putting his ear to his shoulder and then walking past him is an incredibly fast way to gain

---

1. This also works better if your opponent is much larger than you.

control of a situation when someone has just tried to punch you. As you walk past, point to where you want him to fall. Most people will just keel over if you meet the building codes of this move.

When you initially practice this tactic, simply walk past the person and let him fall. Don't try to control the fall just yet. It is crucial first to learn the importance of walking through. One

Incoming punch/parry.

Catch arm/lay head on shoulder.

Walk past.

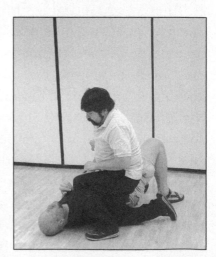

Takedown.

of the most common problems people have in learning this maneuver is that they stop walking forward before the move takes effect. This allows the person to continue to resist. Keep walking past him in order to meet code.

The reason some people stop is, quite simply, because they run out of room. They are so busy focusing on what they are doing with their hands that they are unaware of the obvious fact that they must walk forward on an angle. You don't avoid the person by stepping far out of the way, nor do you walk straight into the person. You pass him and keep going.

Don't worry if at this stage of the game your training partner doesn't fall down, or can still recover. You need to focus more on making sure that your structure and body movement are delivering force and making him hop for balance as you move to a different position. You also need to pay attention to what it feels like when he starts to fall. That is to say, learn to recognize when his structure has been broken and he is keeling over. This is when he will to try to counter the force you are applying. You need to be aware of how that feels, too.

After you have learned to walk past your opponent, it is time to start adding little tweaks that will keep him from countering. The first is designed to keep him from stepping out of the move. You do this by gaffing his arm into your chest or hooking it into your shoulder; either way, pull his arm into you as you walk forward. This pins his arm against a base and doesn't allow him to rotate out of the incoming force. That might not sound like much until you realize that it is his wheeling away from your force that allows him to step and reestablish his base. No wheel, no step; no step, no new base; no reestablishment of structure. Then gravity takes over.

The second tweak comes after you put his ear on his shoulder. Shove it off and try to roll his face into his shoulder blade.

This takes his structure further out of whack and twists him into an even worse position, which prevents him from recovering. Now he can't step or wheel and is twisted in all kinds of unpleasant ways that put him at the mercy of gravity. And if there is anything gravity is short on, it is mercy.

It is important that, though impact can occur while you are moving his head, the move be performed more as a rolling drive. You don't need to hit him. In fact, a hit is often less effective because the opponent has been trained to retract after a blow. This retraction breaks contact and interrupts your force delivery by destroying your structure's connection to him.

The action you want is similar to that of pushing a bowling ball. It's easier, if you push off-center and along the circular shape, instead of trying to push straight through the middle. Trying to roll his head by hitting him dead center is harder than "rolling" it along the outside.

Then you just roll it where you want it to go. Once he runs out of neck, things begin to get complicated for him.

The effect of a twist comes in five basic variations. First, it destroys structural stability. Second, it hyperextends structure and makes it vulnerable to another attack. Third, it sets you up for your next move. Fourth, it takes him off his line of orientation. Fifth, it combines all four of the above.

Notice how the arm is hyperextended and vulnerable to force applied to the elbow. Yes, there could be a strike that breaks the elbow. It could just as easily be a bump of the hip, which would propel him into such objects as walls and tables. Or, when the downward strike is applied to the shoulder, it is an armbar against an uncooperative subject. That is an example of the second and third principles: conditions are developed for your next move to have immediate effect.

Incoming blow.

Trade hands and gaff his arm.

Twist while changing to full grab.

Strike.

I also want you to notice, however, the importance of bringing the twist into a position where you could immediately deliver this force. When you develop twists within the conditions of fence, keep them tight. Do this instead of doing a twist with a chicken wing and dragging it way out yonder. Don't fall into a position where you can't apply force with your next move.

Having said that, the real value of twisting attacks lies with how the attacker is dragged into a teetering position where the rest of his body's structure is compromised and vulnerable. This is a perfect example of the second result: one part of his body is hyperextended, putting the rest of the structure into a precarious position. From that position he is going to have to be more concerned with regaining his balance than with attacking you. Yes, you have his arm, but what is happening to his body is of more use—and easier to exploit. His arm can be the target, but your focus needs to be on exploiting this bigger result, because that is what is guaranteed to end the fight.

The third and fourth results are pure fence. You are in a position where you can attack him but he cannot attack you. You have pulled him in such a way that his orientation is destroyed. Before he can attack you again, he must stop, free himself, regain balance, and reorient.

Once you have your attacker in this position, you have a choice of options. If he is offering severe danger (e.g., wielding a knife) you would be justified in breaking things, like his arm and possibly his neck. If, however, he is not posing severe danger, then by simply pulling or stepping in, you are in perfect position for an armbar or other control tactic.

The handwork for this kind of move is relatively easy if you understand countering and the position you need. Failing to move far enough into the counter will make it nearly impossible. As you enter, you begin to trace your fingers as though you are following a giant wood screw that is pointing toward your armpit. Your fingers trace the thread that spirals down to the point of the screw near your side. This is the type of parrying motion that I mentioned earlier but didn't describe in detail.

The difference is that a circular parry works on centrifugal force. (Imagine a barrel spinning so fast that it looks stationary. What would happen if you touched that barrel with your hand? Your hand would be knocked aside. That's an example of an external circular parry.) This is an internally directed, rather than externally directed, force. The circular or screwing action is more like water going down the drain (centripetal). Anything

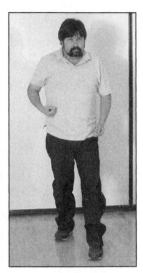

| *Hand out.* | *Pulling back (hand tracing, fingers down).* | *Back palm up.* |

caught in the vortex is sucked in. You catch his limb and suck it into this spiral.

A tweak that makes this move work better is to "pull yourself along the rope." Instead of stepping and then pulling, use him to pull yourself along. Dig your fingers in to gaff him, then pull and use that base to step forward. You not only rocket forward faster, but by using him to pull yourself, you steal his base. You use his structure to speed yourself along and, in so doing, destroy it. He is braced to withstand incoming force, but isn't braced against being jerked forward as you pull yourself past him.

Twisting attacks, whether they involve spinning him around his VA, as I showed in a previous chapter; rolling the head; locking his joint in holds; or pulling him into an armbar position, should all have one major effect: to destroy his orientation. Through either your moving, your moving him, or a combination of the two, he ends up looking in a direction other than where you are. It is better still that he ends up looking somewhere other than where he was originally facing.

Even better is twisting and spinning him, not only along the horizontal plane, but in a three-dimensional manner. You are spinning him around his VA, and also *tipping* his vertical axis. This affects his other axes. Not tipping his axis is far less disorienting than twisting him so that the next thing he knows he is looking at either the floor or the ceiling.

That disorientation buys you all kinds of time, as well as going miles toward taking the fight out of an opponent. Do not underestimate the *"What the hell?"* factor in effective offense. Changing someone's orientation creates confusion that you can use to end violence with minimum violence—especially when he realizes that you are now in a position to hurt him *real bad* if he doesn't knock it off.

The next control technique, although it is a twisting/compressing attack, consists of four drives, a compression, and a pull. See if you can spot them before you read the description. I also want you to see the changes in orientation that have been created.

The first drive moves his arm into his face. This not only destroys his orientation, but prevents him from seeing where you are moving. It also creates a twist that brings his other shoulder forward and in position for your second drive. That drive pushes his shoulder past you as you begin moving into fence. By moving his shoulder to follow his chin, you take his weapons off line. It is now safe for you to move into fence position because you have *cleared the path*. Your upper hand (on his face) checks him from coming back and reorienting on you. As you step into position, you do a double drive (scissoring/compression). Your upper hand drives in a downward diagonal, into his upper torso. Your lower hand is driving through his

Spin the wheel/drunk walk out.

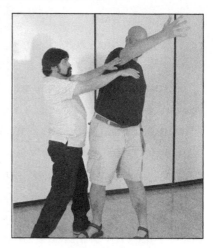

Sweep the path clear.

Left checks his return while right heads to face.

Hand to face, other hand drops to lower back for push.

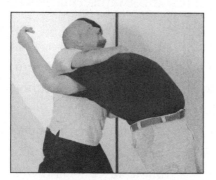

Push and pull (Your hand goes to your opposite shoulder/pulling him into your chest).

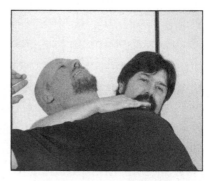

Keeping your arm away from his throat use your chest to steer him and walk him forward.

hips or kidneys, creating a structure-destroying compression attack that moves his hips out from under his shoulders. In the final stage you pull his head and shoulders into your chest (your drive has turned into a pull/compression) while keeping your lower-hand drive out there to prevent him from getting his hips and feet underneath him again.

Right now he has a choice, to cooperate or to hit the deck—hard. Make sure you tell him that, too.

I have used this move countless times to quickly quell a combative person. The bigger and stronger he is, the better it works. That is because of psychology, not physics. A friend of mine got his master's degree in psychology by doing a study about who handled earthquakes the worst. The findings were that large men underwent the greatest stress in earthquakes. Large men were accustomed to picking up and overwhelming other people (and events) through strength. When they found themselves in a tempest in which they were tossed about like leaves in the wind, they were at a loss as to what to do.

That is exactly what this move evokes. Being unexpectedly whipped around and finding oneself in a disoriented, helpless position tends to stop aggressive behavior—until the person can get his *mental feet* under him again. This is why you should immediately start walking them and telling them not to resist, in which case you will have to hurt them. When you do let them go, it is under conditions that you control (e.g., in the presence of backup).

By this time you should begin to see that although there are six different types of attack in Dr. Pitt & Co, there is a lot of overlap among them. You should also have begun to realize that most effective attacks are not a single manifestation (e.g., impact). Attacks that combine several aspects are far more effective.

This leads us to the final component of Dr. Pitt & Co, takedowns. I break takedowns into two basic categories, throws and takedowns. A throw is what most people think of when they think of judo. You pick a person up and hurl him, preventing him from reestablishing his base. These you can learn through any throwing art so I won't go into them.

A takedown is different from a throw because it relies on gravity, off-balancing, and countering. It can take the form of an actual hands-on dropping of an opponent, a sweep, or one of a variety of other options that aren't exactly throws. While you can get away with a throw by being bigger and stronger than your opponent, a takedown relies on your being in the right place.

The Big 3 of range, body movement, and structure are fundamental to making a takedown work. More than with other moves, you must be where you need to be. If you are not in the right place, you will not be able to exploit the IBR that you create—nor will you be able to stop his counter.

That simple statement is why most takedowns or throws fail.

Although the summation is simple, the reasons behind it are complex because you have two variable programs going on at once: yours and his. Your actions must address both.

The first variable you must address are the almost instinctive reactions humans have regarding loss of balance. I say "instinctive" because they are automatic responses that you must counter in order to succeed. Unless people are very, very drunk, well-trained, or so oriented toward killing you that they don't bother to react, these will be their reactions to a loss of balance. Once you know them, you will begin to see how often they interfere with takedowns or throws.

When people stumble, their first, natural (and very fast) reaction is to try to put their foot out in order to reestablish structure. They may not get their balance back, but with a foot underneath them they can teeter and try to regain it. This happens so fast because it is a natural part of walking. We have been doing it since we learned how to walk. If you have ever tripped over a crack, you have done this yourself; your foot automatically shoots out in order to keep you from falling. Most often this is accompanied with the hands going out to help find balance.

The second reaction happens if the first fails, which is to try to grab onto something. While it can be a part of the first response (waving your arms to keep balance), those outstretched hands grab. In this case the person grabs to steal structure from something nearby and hangs on in order to keep from falling. Bad news: the only thing handy to grab is you.

The third reaction is to reach out and soften the impact. That's why your palms get scraped when you fall.

If you need to neutralize a serious threat, you don't want your opponent to have a chance to do any of the three. You want him to hit full force and shatter.

If you are trying to control him, however, you don't want him to have a chance to do anything except the third. Unfortunately, the way most people try to do takedowns and throws gives their opponent a chance to do everything else—except the third and they don't need the third because they aren't going down, or if they are they are taking you with them.

The reason most takedowns don't work (or become wrestling matches) is that the person either steps and reestablishes his base or grabs onto the closest thing available: you!

This can succeed if the person attempting to execute a takedown fails to prevent these automatic reactions. Although failing to break his structure or balance is a common problem, if you watch you will generally see that it was broken—initially. What the thrower didn't do was prevent his opponent from reestablishing it.

Yes, he moved him, but because he didn't prevent him from stepping, he allowed him to reestablish structure with that step! Then the contest becomes one of strength and mass. Yeah, the thrower made the guy almost fall. But he didn't change his orientation in order to keep him from grabbing on and dragging the thrower down with him. In either case the person doing the takedown didn't check the automatic counter/IBR, the very thing that he created.

The reason the opponent can return to structure is because the person doing the takedown or throw often doesn't understand that it is not a single move, nor is it several separate moves. It is a sequential process of several phases.

There is a big difference in timing. In moves that involve a *single body movement*, all you do is one kind of movement and that is it. That single move (e.g., step forward and shove) powers what you are doing.

Other moves involve *combined movement*, whereby you do two movements at once. A good example is pivoting as you bend your knees (turn, kneel, and pray). This combines a circular move with a downward action (downward screwing).

There is, however, a third category, what I call *sequential movement*. This is not two separate moves. You don't (1) move, (2) stop, and then (3) move again. Sequential movement is one move that is a two-step process (1ab). There is no pause between the two actions, but neither are the actions simultaneous. The moves flow into one another.

The best way to explain this concept is with three marking pens that have interconnecting lids and bottoms. One pen is a single body movement (like walking). If you hold all three bundled up in your hand, that is combined (three different moves happening at once). Lay the markers in a row with spaces between the cap of one and the bottom of the next. This is *not* sequential movement. It is three single moves occurring one after another. Take those three markers and connect them so that the cap of one plugs into the bottom of the next. What you should now have is one stick with three distinct parts. Parts that meld one into the other. This is sequential movement. The power of one is transferred into, and increased by, the power of the next. The three moves are not separated, nor do they occur simultaneously. By analyzing all the moves in your system using this model you will be able to communicate to your students the correct method of movement far more effectively and quickly.

For a perfect example, let's look at the basic hit. Pick any hit you want and go to the heavy bag, but stand back, slightly out of range. A punch is a sequential move (1ab) because it has two parts. First, you step into range (a). By doing so, you transfer your body weight forward. (This is a single body movement). By now you should not be stepping straight in, but at a slight angle. Near the end of the weight transfer, however, you begin to twist your hips (b). This accelerates your body's momentum and allows you to hit harder. It also redirects your force directly into his VA.

This is a "1ab" move. You do not stop between actions, i.e., you do not make them two separate actions (e.g., step and transfer weight, stop, then pivot). Nor do you do both at once (e.g., start the step and twist at the same time). Try hitting both ways on the bag and see why you shouldn't do so.

Sequential moves don't just flow into one another; they are parts of the same move. While they can happen so close to each other that they are nearly indistinguishable, they are not an homogenized (or combined) whole.

I want you to recognize the power of this tool—not only for learning, but for teaching, as well. Recently, I had a chance to work out with a muay Thai coach in Utah. This man has over 200 professional fights under his belt, most of them in his native Thailand. When he kicks a bag, the entire building shakes. Watching him move provided a study in sequential movement, weight transfer, and structure. What was most gratifying, however, was his students' reaction after I showed them the three kinds of timing—how much more in awe of him they were after they understood his mastery. He, in turn, was ecstatic that his students' finally understood what he was trying to teach them about timing.

The reason I bring up this model of the three types of timing is to point out that a takedown or throw involves sequential timing. It is a two-step process. To make the whole work, the two parts must be completed. The two steps are simple: (1) break his structure/balance, and (2) make sure that he doesn't reestablish structure or counter.

Simply stated, once you break it, don't let them fix it.

All you need to do is move him to a point where he is teetering and then push an extra inch. The hard part is making sure that he can't wiggle out of the result.

Notice that I didn't say, "The hard part is making sure that he can't resist you." That would amount to a fight in which you are actively attempting to overcome his counters. That is why so many people try to use throws. You pick him up and throw him before he can do anything to reestablish his structure and resist. The problem is, you are working so hard that you won't stop all the ways in which he can resist. You took care of the first counter, but got dragged over by the second.

I said that a good offense is like a bureaucracy from hell because it just gets in the way of his doing anything. It keeps him so busy dealing with those problems that he doesn't have time to attack you. What I am talking about gives him a far more immediate problem: gravity. You become secondary, because not falling is his most pressing problem. Unfortunately for him it's hard to prevent himself from falling because you are in his way. This ability to counter his attempts to keep from falling is a byproduct of your being in the right place or, in other words, of fence.

It is a law of physics that two objects cannot occupy the same space at the same time. If you are there, he has problems. If you are not in the correct location, however, you will not be able to check him and he will reestablish structure. When that happens, it turns into a contest of muscle and mass.

Keeping what I have just said in mind, I would like you to re-examine the contention that in order to fight, you must be in top physical condition. Unfortunately, the way people use this idea is putting the cart before the horse and then insisting that you carry the horse. Their thinking goes like this. *In order to compensate for being in the wrong place, I have to be in good physical condition so that I can pick him up and throw him before he starts to resist.*

That attitude is fine and dandy until you go up against someone who is bigger and stronger than you are. Then it becomes a contest of strength and endurance in which both parties usually end up falling to the ground and wrestling.

What I have just said is in fact extremely controversial, especially among people who believe that physical conditioning is the foundation of good fighting skills. Unfortunately, all too often such people train to the exclusion of other critical aspects, like moving into fence.

For the record let me say that, yes, physical conditioning is a very important aspect of sports fighting, a limited-offense situation in which your goal is not to end the contest per se, but to win it. You will need to be able to take punishment and to last a long time. Physical conditioning is also very important to police or military personnel who might be called upon to function for long periods of time without sleep and under strenuous conditions. And after which they must still have the ability to fight and function appropriately (e.g., to chase a "perp" on foot and then subdue him).

I will also be so bold as to say that physical conditioning can assist you in prevailing against either an untrained opponent or a so-called trained opponent whose actions don't meet the building codes. You can overwhelm him with sheer mass and muscle.

What physical conditioning won't do is compensate for a lack of skill against a larger, stronger, armed, or more skillful opponent, or multiple opponents. Because of the damage you will take in doing so, conditioning is only of marginal use for these kinds of opponents. In that case, all you do in hang on and let him beat on you until he tires out, as long as he doesn't have a weapon.

In no other type of attack is an ingrained understanding of fence more important than a takedown. You must be in a position—or must move him into a position—where he has no chance to reestablish his structure. If you don't, he will.

This goes double if you have moved into a location and then stopped. You need to keep moving, not only because it gives you an endless supply of power, but because of where he needs to be in order to resist keeps changing. Yes, he found a position to resist you, but that was eight inches back. Now he needs to be somewhere else. Oops, too bad he didn't get there in time.

Directional change, movement, and force directed continually in downward diagonal ways tend to keep opponents from effectively reestablishing their structure. But what about grabbing on? Again, you already have the answer and the tool to counter it: orientation and twisting.

When you twist someone away from you while at the same time driving him in another direction, you greatly reduce his chances of grabbing onto you when his attempts to reestablish structure fail. In order to grab you, he has to know where you are. If he is spinning like a top, that task is much harder.

Take another look at the control tactic I showed you earlier, and see how it can work.

If instead of pulling him into you, you continue to drive him down while spinning him, he will fall into what LEOs call a *cuffing position*, that is, lying on his stomach.

Several variations of this move will put him into this position. In one, you pull him into your chest, then step back, pivot, and kneel. This downward spiraling motion tends to wing his arm up into you for an armbar. In another variation, instead of pulling him into your chest, keep the spin going and do the diagonal drive perpendicular to your chest, near the end of the drive; turn in the same direction; step; and kneel. This, too, often results in his arm flying up into your waiting hand for an armbar.

Care must be taken, however, if after the second spinning drive you simply hook onto his shoulder and step back and kneel. This is a faster and harder takedown, which slams him

In your face.

Step in.

Set up your pull.

Pull him into you.

Start to spin.

Move left hand up to shoulder for drive and take him down.

down with greater force. If you are attempting to control a particularly violent person, you should cup the back of his head in your hand, in order to protect it from hitting the ground. From there you just clamp your other hand on his face and twist. The person will roll over into a cuffing position.

This move can become lethal if you don't take safety precautions and accelerate his fall. That is something you should do only when lethal force is legally justified (e.g., if he has a knife and has just tried to gut you). If you do that under any other circumstances, you will be looking at a prison sentence for manslaughter.

These are just some of the ways that Dr. Pitt & Co can be used to make sure that you not only meet code, but exceed it. This is how, with three moves, you can make sure that an opponent is off his feet and unable to attack. You want each of your moves to do at least three things. Your three moves have the same value as nine of his. When your moves become effective, you will find that you have greater faith in your abilities, and adrenaline rushes will become far less of an issue. You will have greater control over your reactions and how much damage you do, while still being effective.

The more effective you are, the less force you will need to use.

~ 14 ~

In Closing

The general who wins a battle makes many calculations in his temple 'ere the battle is fought.

The general who loses a battle makes but few calculations beforehand.

Thus do many calculations lead to victory, few calculations to defeat: how much more no calculations at all!

It is by attention to this point that I can foresee who is likely to win or lose.

—Sun Tzu, *The Art of War*

People ask me if I am a martial artist.

No, I am not. I tell them that I am a martial analyst.

People ask me what fighting style I use.

I don't have one. I have a training style. It not only helps me be a better fighter, but allows the people I teach to think for themselves and fight well.

People ask me what my favorite fighting technique is.

My answer is, whatever is necessary.

In Closing

What I do in conflict depends on what is happening, not what martial arts style I know. The technique that I use is whatever works best to achieve my goal of ending it quickly, at that exact moment. The next moment, I will be doing something completely different. What I can tell you is that whatever I do is based on the fundamentals and principles I have spoken about in this book.

This attitude is so ingrained that I often cannot tell you exactly how I did something. In seminars, someone will attack and I will counter. When participants ask me to demonstrate the technique I just did, I have to tell them, "That was so five seconds ago."

This confuses them because didn't I just do it?

Well, yes, but I was so focused on getting to the goal that I didn't pay attention to exactly how I got there. Does a soldier advancing under fire pay attention to every step that he takes? No, he doesn't. He is more focused on achieving certain steps that will lead him to a greater goal. The details of how to move with his equipment have long ago been addressed in boot camp. He has ingrained them so that he just moves that way. This frees his mind to work toward his larger, strategic goals.

While this may sound appalling to people who want the chaos of battle to fit in a nice, comfortable little box, I can assure you that successes in battle isn't about techniques, but about strategy. More important, it is about being able to tailor general strategy into tactics appropriate for the circumstances; specific tactics that work toward the greater strategic goal.

There is a serious misconception in modern training tactics: just knowing a technique means that you also know when, where, and how to apply it. *This is not true.* In order to know when to apply it strategically, you must study strategy.

Unfortunately, an equally flawed theory has arisen: getting the details of a technique down is not nearly as important as doing it with gusto. Again, I say that it doesn't matter how fast you get somewhere if you arrive at the wrong place. But this time I can add, "Or if you don't have anything when you get there." Getting there "the furstest with the leastest" is not a winning strategy.

As with anything, there is no single answer. Effective offense is largely based on effective training. By this I mean training that encompasses many aspects beyond just the physical. If there is an art to martial, it comes from knowing how and when to apply resources in order to achieve your strategic goals under less than ideal circumstances.

To make someone effective in combat, many factors must blend. This includes having ingrained the building codes of a move to the point where you don't have to think about how to do it. You automatically do it correctly. It also includes understanding the reason why certain aspects need to be given priority, and understanding that, when it comes down to it, nobody can keep you from achieving these goals. There are incredible psychological factors involved, too, from having faith in these priorities so that you can act with commitment, to learning the forensic art of thinking strategically. Physiological and spiritual factors come into the picture, as well, from knowing the effects of adrenalin on both your mind and body to having an indomitable spirit. Legal issues pervade this subject, such as knowing when it is time to stop and having the self-control to do so, as does the matter of training under high-stress conditions so that you can operate under live-fire circumstances.

These and countless other issues are involved in effective offense. Unfortunately, they are not addressed by any single training method or fighting style. That means that you have a lot of research and work ahead of you.

In summation, I want to give you an idea of what it takes to be an effective fighter: You must be a general, not a grunt.

The forces that you command are yours, and you must take care to understand that their marshaling, deployment, and strategic use are under your command. If you don't command them, they will run wild. You must develop the skills necessary to deploy your troops effectively in order to achieve victory.

On the subject of being a warrior, many people in the martial arts like to quote Miyamoto Musashi in his *Book of Five Rings*. When it comes to ensuring your personal safety, I'm not much of a fan of Musashi, for the same reason that I don't have much respect for the guy on the loading dock who is preaching about how the company should be run. While it is important that he does his job and does it well, that is only one aspect of what it takes to run a successful company. The "warrior" mindset is good for getting the job done, but it is not the same as the strategic mind, which is what it takes to define the job that must be done and the best way to do it.

Hand-to-hand combat is very much like a small war. You must deploy your resources under extremely adverse conditions and against an opponent who is trying to do the same to you. The side that does so most skillfully will be the winner.

This is why most of the chapter quotes in this book come not from famous "martial artists," but from men with actual experience in warfare. These men dedicated their lives to the art and science of war. They knew what it took to be successful in that arena. In closing, I would like to leave you with more quotes and thought-provoking comments by these men, who are not only warriors, but strategists.

> "In critical and baffling situations it is always best
> to return to first principle and simple action."
> —Winston Churchill

"The victorious strategist only seeks battle after the victory has been won, whereas he who is destined to defeat first fights and afterwards looks for victory."—Sun Tzu, *The Art of War*, translated by Lionel Giles

"To apply one's strength where the opponent is strong weakens oneself disproportionately to the effect attained. To strike with strong effect, one must strike at weakness."—Sir Basil H. Liddel-Hart, *Strategy*

"Being ready is not what matters. What matters is winning after you get there."—Lt. Gen. V. H. Krulak, U.S. Marine Corps

"In no other profession are the penalties for employing untrained personnel so appalling or so irrevocable as in the military."—Gen. Douglas MacArthur

"A good plan, violently executed now, is better than a perfect plan next week."—Gen. George S. Patton

"The good fighters of old first put themselves beyond the possibility of defeat, and then waited for an opportunity of defeating the enemy. To secure ourselves against defeat lies in our own hands, but the opportunity of defeating the enemy is provided by the enemy himself. Thus the good fighter is able to secure himself against defeat, but cannot make certain of defeating the enemy."—Sun Tzu

"Take time to deliberate, but when the time for action has arrived, stop thinking and go in."—Napoleon Bonaparte

"Watch what people are cynical about, and one can often discover what they lack."—Gen. George S. Patton

"It is folly to imagine that the aggressive types can be bought off, whether nations or individuals . . . since the payment of 'Danegeld' stimulates the demand for more Danegeld. But they can be curbed. Their very belief in force makes them more susceptible to the deterrent effect of a formidable opposing force."—Sir Basil H. Liddel-Hart

"The most consistently successful commanders, when faced by an enemy in a position that was strong naturally or materially, have hardly ever tackled it in a direct way. And when under pressure of circumstances, they have risked a direct attack, the result has commonly been to blot their record with a failure."—Sir Basil H. Liddel-Hart

"So in the war, the way is to avoid what is strong and to strike at what is weak."—Sun Tzu

"It is thus more potent, as well as more economical, to disarm the enemy than to attempt his destruction by hard fighting . . . A strategist should think in terms of paralyzing, not of killing."—Sir Basil H. Liddel-Hart

"The art of war teaches us to rely not on the likelihood of the enemy's not coming, but on our own readiness to receive him; not on the chance of his not attacking, but rather on the fact that we have made our position unassailable."—Sun Tzu

"Success demands a high level of logistical and organizational competence."—Gen. George S. Patton

"Unhappy is the fate of one who tries to win his battles and succeed in his attacks without cultivating the spirit of enterprise; for the result is waste of time and general stagnation. Hence the saying: 'The enlightened ruler lays his plans well ahead; the good general cultivates his resources.'"—Sun Tzu

"Bravery without forethought causes a man to fight blindly and desperately like a mad bull. Such an opponent must not be encountered with brute force, but may be lured into an ambush and slain."—Ts'ao Kung

"People who have not seen death should not make war, especially when they are too proud to learn."
—Gen. George S. Patton

"Ah gets there tha furstest with tha mostest."
—attributed to Nathan Bedford Forrest

Appendix: An Example of Coherent Body Movement

As I said earlier, the most fundamental version of coherent body movement is evident when the hips and shoulders move together. While this concept is well known in karate and similar arts, I would like to introduce you to an effective way of doing it called the "drop step"—or at least that is what Jack Dempsey called it.

Unfortunately, Dempsey's book *Championship Fighting* is out of print and harder to find than an honest politician. In case you are not familiar with Mr. Dempsey's record, he was boxing's world heavyweight champion in the 1920s. Of his sixty-four title fights, he won sixty by knockout. The shortest bout lasted fourteen seconds before his opponent was unconscious on the ring floor. So, claims of the effectiveness of ancient and secret Asian fighting systems aside, the "Manassa Mauler" knew a thing or two about power delivery.

Having said that, I would like to add that I was a young buck when I first read Dempsey's book. (It was written in 1950 and republished in 1983). I used it many times and with great success over decades of professional use of force (defensive tactics/CQC (close quarter combat), etc.). So I can personally attest to its effectiveness outside the boxing ring, as can many of the professionals whom I have trained. We'll just assume that the people who ended up on the floor, wondering what hit them, won't want to testify—but they are out there, too.

Simply stand normally and start a forward motion from your hips instead of your chest. Don't lean forward; your hips will "fall forward off your thighs." In order to catch yourself, you will have to bend your knees and do an exaggerated stomp.

Your vertical axis should stay vertical. In this initial phase, you don't want to bend or twist; just shift your weight forward and stomp. Moving in this manner creates an avalanche effect, as it puts a majority of your mass in motion all at once. Don't do this just a few times, but spend at least an hour practicing various degrees of the "drop" by experimenting with how long your stride is and how deeply you bend your knees. A drop step can cover as much as four feet or as little as a few inches.

Once you have the basic move down, modify it so that all of your weight is on the front foot. You can test this by assuming what I call the "cheesy movie kiss" position. Check to see if you have put all your weight on your front foot by lifting your back leg.

This ensures that all of your weight is going forward and stopping in the correct place, i.e., your body movement is coherent. You should be able to easily lift your foot without balancing or any other weight shifting. If you need to counterbalance, keep practicing, because you are not in the right place.

Once you can easily put your weight over your front foot every time, you can begin to experiment with different proportions, such as 80–20 or 70–30. However, before you try this you should be able to "walk across the room" with one drop step after another, just by shooting forward your "kissing" leg and falling into the next drop step.

You can test the efficiency of the drop step with a few training partners. Have one partner stand in front of you and another behind him, to "catch." It is best if the person being "pushed" doesn't try to resist. In fact, it is even better if he wears some kind of chest protection or, at the very least, holds a large phone book tightly against his chest.

Step forward as you normally do and "push" the first training partner into the catcher. Don't try to muscle him; just use your forward momentum.

For the second part, do the drop step while keeping your elbows down to your side. As your foot hits the ground, snap your hands out into the push. If your timing is anywhere close, your partner should be "blown" back into the catcher's arm.

Don't try to do anything to enhance this exercise. Don't try to do it faster or harder; just drop step and shoot your hands out. The power is already there; the trick is learning how to deliver it. It is critical that you learn how to generate power from coherent body movement before you try to enhance it. Most attempts to make it "stronger" will actually rob you of power. Take turns so that each of you can feel the difference in power.

Another important exercise is learning how to do the drop step in any direction. I would recommend starting with the easiest of the alternate directions, backward. Without tilting your VA, just sit back, as though you were falling onto a comfortable couch. Before you would be caught by the imaginary couch, shoot your leg out and down behind you, so that you end up sitting on your leg.

Now begin to make the drop step go in all directions. With practice you should be able to drop step anywhere on a 360-degree circle. When moving in any direction other than forward or backward, I suggest that you have a partner present (and, if possible, filming you). His observation will alert you to the two most common errors in drop stepping in other directions: hopping and rocking.

When they first try this, most people tend to "pony step" or "frog hop" to the side. This means that they "jump." Your head should simply slide down a diagonal line, from where it was into the new position. If you hop, your head will trace an arc into the new position. This is ineffective and is a subconscious control element. We humans don't like falling, so we tend to jump. This amounts to extra movement.

Another form of extra movement is "rocking." Your head should go from the noon position on a taller clock to noon on a shorter clock next to it. It should not rock back to 11:30 on the original clock. If it does, you are transferring your weight to one leg and then stepping where you are going, instead of just "dropping" into the new position.

Your training partner is there to prevent you from adding in these unconscious "extra steps," which will rob you of power and coherence of movement.

As I said, don't try to enhance these moves, just learn how to do them efficiently. These exercises are not fighting applications or drills. They are basic exercises designed to teach body motion. Body motions are integral to effective offense, but as they are often hurriedly studied in order to get to the "good stuff," they are poorly understood.

The ability to launch an effective offense is predicated *on having these elements present in every move you do*. Without them, you are just waving your arms. They will only become automatic if you practice with them in mind.

Having said that, if you want to combine two exercises, try doing the drop step into the range of the hanging bag. Practice the different size steps to get into range to touch the bag's VA. Repeatedly doing these exercises for an hour a day for two weeks may not impress the women, but all the guys will be wondering how you are hitting that bag so hard.

Once you have these basic elements down, you can begin working to enhance them. The key word is *enhance*.

Many people go wrong by attempting to make the enhancements the source of their power, rather than a supplement it.

This brings us to the last aspect of body movement: acceleration. I hope everyone realizes that what I have been talking about all along is moving your body into range for your offense. That is the basic version. The more advanced version is that you have been using coherent body movement to move into fence. You're not attacking yet, but you have set up the staging area so that you can attack him, but he can't attack you. When you accelerate that, it really becomes offensive.

Watch a boxer. You will see that he steps into range, twists his hips, and then shoots the punch. Well, in truth, he moves into range and twists his leg. That causes his hip to twist during the last stage of the weight transfer, which in turn shoots his punch. This sequence is very, very important.

In a sports context, generating momentum by stepping into range is all precursor work. In most people's eyes, the attack hasn't been launched yet. In a shortsighted way, this is true. They see the attack as being launched only when the fist is flying toward its target because . . . well . . . that's the most obvious manifestation. They can see it.

Then again, it is also pretty easy at the last second to see the semi that is about to run you over. That doesn't explain how it got there or how it managed to be going so fast.

In truth, the boxer's attack began with his stepping into range. This is why I say that you can throw fast punches or you can throw powerful punches, but you can't do both. A fast "sports" punch consists only of sticking your fist out. It's pure muscle and speed; there is no body movement. Range doesn't matter, as long as the punch lands. And yes, it is fast and it looks great. It doesn't, however, deliver your power into your opponent.

Powerful blows take longer. You need to do at least three things. First, you must position your body so that you can throw a move with structure. Second, you must move into range. Third, you must transfer your weight. Finally, as icing on the cake, you accelerate the whole package. Somewhere near the end of all that, you actually stick your fist out.

I mentioned that this is in a sports context. Generally, when you are in a limited-offense situation like sports, you have to worry only about moving to where you can touch your opponent. However, when dealing with unlimited or total offense, your moving into range must be an integral part of moving into fence. It is during fence that you off-balance him, twist him, and set him up for your actual offense.

It is from this position that your body's acceleration launches what most people think of as the "attack." But this should not occur until you have all your ducks in a row. It is from the safety of fence that your hip-twists, directional changes, seating, wiggling, pelvic thrusts, coiling, or other actions accelerate your existing momentum. These moves are not the source of your power; they make what you have better.

By trying to make your turning hips the "source" of your power, most of the time you end up losing power because you "split" your line of force instead of making it bigger.

Let me give you a series of exercises to illustrate what I am talking about. Go to the heavy bag, wearing hand wraps. You will be throwing a hook. A few of these are not going to work, but be patient. Stand in the range of the hook. Now, without twisting your hips, try to throw a hook into the bag's VA. This is nothing but arm, but try to hit it as fast as you can.

Step back. While stepping into range, but without turning your hips, throw another hook. It is very important that you avoid throwing the hips into this blow. Try to throw a hook without a circular body movement, instead making a straight movement.

Now, staying in range but without making any forward movement, throw another hook, turning your hips into it. This will be by far the most powerful blow you have thrown in the exercise.

You have isolated various elements and seen how they work individually. I want you now to step back out of range. Step into range and—this is very important—without arresting your forward momentum, twist your hips into the hook. You will move into range, take your forward momentum, and "sling" it into the hook.

The timing shouldn't be "step, twist, hook." That is three separate actions. Nor should it be three things mixed up as one. It should be one move with three different parts. It should be "steptwisthook."

Now *that's* a hit!

The increased magnitude of the blow should shock you. That's because you are using your hips not as the "source" of the power, but as an acceleration of your existing momentum. Remember how I said that momentum equals mass times velocity? By doing it this way, your hips increase your mass's velocity. It doesn't have to be a big twist; in fact, the smaller the better. It doesn't take much, just a small "snap" to greatly increase your velocity.

But here is where most people end up robbing themselves of energy by trying to make their power come from enhancements. They either overdo the hip twist, wait too long to do it, or try to do it all at once. The first sends the energy off into another direction. The second loses the forward momentum and then tries to re-create momentum from the hip twist. The last, while useful in the proper context, isn't very good for striking.

I want you to hit the bag again, but in a different manner. As you step, twist at the same time. Your foot and the hook should hit at the same time that you are stepping and twisting. Don't be surprised if you end up stumbling. This is hitting in the last manner I just spoke about, where everything happens at once.

Let's say we have an imaginary boxer who just did the preceding exercise. His body was originally moving at 10 miles an hour as he moved forward into range. Let's say that he weighs 175 pounds. This means that he had the potential of delivering 1,750 pounds of pressure. Without twisting his hips, however, the angle is wrong for delivering the power of the hook. This means that he had no structure and his energy functionally bled away (as with the exercise you did earlier, involving a hook thrown with forward momentum only). Now, had he done the same forward motion with a jab, it would have been a different story.

When he was not moving forward but twisted his hips, let's say—for ease of explanation—that he was again moving at 10 mph. Now he had that 1,750 pounds of pressure going into the bag (as in the hip-twist-without-forward-momentum exercise).

But by joining them "sequentially," he takes the original 10 mph and adds the 10 mph of the twist, so when his blow lands he is in fact moving at 20 mph. This would give him a net force of 3,500 pounds of pressure, and that force is all channeled right where he wants it to go (as in the moving-into-range-and-accelerating-with-the-hips exercise).

This is in stark contrast to the last attempt. By stepping and twisting at the same time, he hasn't increased his "deliverable momentum." What he has in essence done is put a "spin" on his forward momentum and split his line of force.

Yes, there is extra momentum there, but it is neither controlled or channeled. Like the "glass" tipped from the table, it is moving in multiple directions. Therefore, when that movement encounters resistance (hits the target), it will become a wild card—a force that is more likely to backfire than assist you, as you probably found out when you did the exercise. By the way, it is not unusual for people to stumble when they hit that way.

Such an event is what I refer to as "splitting your lines of force," or what Steve Plinck refers to as "moving two bases at one time" (i.e., the feet and the shoulders). It is a common problem when people try to create power built on "enhancers." You end up destroying your coherent body movement and scattering your momentum to the four corners.

You can tell when you are splitting your lines of force because, instead of "hitting" the bag, you will either bounce off it or, in essence, slap it. While a slap, correctly done, can create an incredible amount of energy transfer, in this case the only mass involved in the strike is your hand. And as you have seen, speed without mass is of very little value (as in hitting the bag without twisting your hips).

It doesn't really matter what system or style you know or practice. These five elements will somehow be there. Various styles manifest these elements differently, based on the type of body movement (power generation) that a given system uses. How your system generates power is less important than that these elements are always present in your body movement and offense.

By the way, I want you to notice something. Boxers don't always step into range. A lot of the time, they let their opponent step into range, and thereby the other fellow provides the momentum. The boxer just supplies the structure for the other fellow to break his face on. But in order to do this, you must have a very good understanding of range and structure.

Acknowledgments

No idea, no matter how brilliant, original, or practical, comes into this world complete and on its own. There are always foundations, connections, prior teachings, assisting knowledge, and history. And no system is complete and workable until it has been checked, tested, and peer reviewed—and then proven in the big bad world. Over the years I have had teachers, friends, and colleagues who helped me understand what is involved in effective offense. In recent years they have contributed to this effort by showing me where I am wrong and what I have forgotten or overlooked, by offering myriad different ways to do things, and by pointing out legal and psychological implications. Their help has been invaluable. I cannot thank them enough, but I can acknowledge how much the following people have helped me.

First, foremost, and above all, my wife, Dianna Gordon MacYoung, cofounder of Dango Jiru and editor of both my writing and my scattered thought processes.

Tristan Sutrisno, 8th dan karate, dan Kinjitsu, dan Aikido, and murid Tjimande. Rangers lead the way. Thank you, bro; you inspire me to look for the next set of mountains.

Ernie "Oberon" Selicio, who took a scared street punk and showed me the realities of fighting, as well as the fact that it is about so much more.

Sifu Hawkins Cheung, who introduced me to Wing Chun and whose teachings saved my life on many occasions—even if it would be years before I understood them.

Dr. Alex Holub, sifu Five Family Gung Fu, Ph.D. psychology. As always, Alf meets the Terminator.

Stevan Plinck, guru Pukulan Pentjak Silat Serak, who, while he wasn't able to teach me serak, helped me return to the fundamentals with awe-inspiring new perspective.

Justin Kocher, 2 dan Danzan Ryu, for his longtime friendship and ability to sum up my babbling, incoherent ideas in simple, consise terms.

Dr. Joseph Bablonaka, 5th dan Tang So Do, 6th Rossi Kuntao, Ph.D. psychology.

Tim Toohey, Detroit streetfighter, Brown Water Navy. I miss you, bro.

Bob Orlando, guru, sifu, and possessor of a fine analytical mind . . . even if he is a Marine.

Peyton Quinn, RMCAT founder. It takes serious brilliance to keep it that simple.

Alain Burrese, sabunim, Hapkido, author, sniper, instructor, and friend . . . even if he is a lawyer.

Masaad Ayoob, Lethal Force Institute, Judicious Use of Lethal Force instructor.

Col. Rex Applegate, whose World War II combatives saved my young life many a time.

Sifu Frank "Pancho" Garza, Kenpo, USMC, and "Pancho Fu." Each head is a world unto itself.

Slavo Gozdznik, founder, Explosive Self-Defense, and head of International Police Defensive Tactics.

Chris Carracci, SEAL Team 6, Gunsite instructor, LEO . . . and not someone I would want to point a gun at me.

Rick Hernandez, professor, Kuntao. My wife still thinks we're East and West Coast versions of each other.

David "Doc" Marks, my oldest living friend, who always makes me think about what I am saying.

Gila and Marty Hayes, Firearms Academy of Seattle.

Sifu Karl Totten, who introduced me to the power of "soft styles."

Craig Lamana, muay Thai of Kunupali and the person who helps me keep it real.

Sakasem Kathawong, who, aside from being poetry in motion, finally taught me how to throw a kick with power.

Lt. Col. Dave Grossman, author, warrior, and founder of Killology research.

Terry Trahan, who by teaching, I remembered.

Wim Demeere, coach, Belgium Wushu national team.

William "Buzz" Lange, who taught me to always keep the runway in front.

Jesse and Page Alcorta, sabumin, whose arguments and analysis have helped me greatly. And who helped provide photographs for this book.

Rick Foss, who always showed me the other side of the argument.

Stewart McArthur Burnett, my grandfather, who taught me, "You can figure out anything if you just look at it long enough."

Dr. Stanton Samenow, author, *Inside the Criminal Mind*.

Dr. Drew Anderson, SUNY Albany, who helped me understand about learning.

Dr. Eric Shaver, ergonomic psychology, who helps me remember that it isn't just common sense.

Doug Wittrock, gentle giant, paramedic extraordinaire, and uke for this book.

Acknowledgments

Ian Hogan, Oppugnate Australia. Celtic warrior, scholar, and all-around good mate.

Paul Spiegel, attorney. If you think I'm nasty, you oughta meet my lawyer.

Members of the "Animal List," who constantly remind me that I don't know it all and that friendship is far more important than fame.

About the Author

Marc MacYoung is an internationally renowned personal safety instructor and the author of several books on the subject. He lives in Colorado when not presenting seminars in Europe, North America, and Asia.

Index

Index

Index